Superintendent's Handbook
of Financial Management

Superintendent's Handbook of Financial Management

Revised Edition

Raymond S. Schmidgall

WILEY

John Wiley & Sons, Inc.

This book is printed on acid-free paper. ∞

Copyright © 2004 by John Wiley & Sons, Inc. All rights reserved.

Published by John Wiley & Sons, Inc., Hoboken, New Jersey
Published simultaneously in Canada

For general information on our other products and services or for technical support, please contact our
Customer Care Department within the United States at (800) 762-2974, outside the United States at
(317) 572-3993 or fax (317) 572-4002.

Wiley also publishes its books in a variety of electronic formats. Some content that appears in print may
not be available in electronic books. For more information about Wiley products, visit our web site at
www.wiley.com.

Library of Congress Cataloging-in-Publication Data:
Schmidgall, Raymond S., 1945-
  Superintendent's handbook of financial management / by Raymond
Schmidgall.— 2nd ed.
     p. cm.
Includes index.
   ISBN 0-471-46319-1 (Cloth : alk. paper)
   1. Golf courses—Finance. 2. Managerial accounting. I. Title.
   GV975.S25 2003
   796.352'06'91—dc21
                              2003003580

PRINTED IN THE UNITED STATES OF AMERICA
10 9 8 7 6 5 4

Contents

3

Basic Accounting Procedures and Records   **35**

4

Golf Course Operations Schedule   **59**

5

Analysis of Financial Statements   **77**

6

7

8

9

Preface

This book is written both to acquaint the golf course superintendent with financial management concepts and to serve as a guide for studying for the financial management section of the Golf Course Superintendents Association of America's certification examination.

The emphasis on the certification examination is the major concepts covered in the nine chapters. Though concepts from each chapter are covered on the certification exam, *the concepts of chapters five and six are less emphasized than the remaining chapters.*

This book is the responsibility of its author; however, the certification committee members of GCSAA served as reviewers of the chapter contents for the initial edition. In addition, Cleve Cleveland, CGCS, CPA of the Newark Valley Golf Club, Inc. and Frank Agnello of the Oakland Hills Country Club also provided several helpful suggestions that were included in the production of the original book.

John O'Donnell, general manager of the Detroit Golf Club provided the 2000 Annual Report of the Detroit Golf Club. Autumn Keller, sales administrator of Weingartz Golf and Turf, provided a sales quote on a John Deere fairway mower. Both of these documents were incorporated in the revised edition.

I trust this book will be most helpful in expanding your knowledge of financial management for golf courses and in your passing the financial management section of the certification examination.

RAYMOND S. SCHMIDGALL
Hilton Hotels Professor
Michigan State University

1

Introduction to Financial Management

This chapter introduces the subject of financial management as it applies to the management of golf course operations.

A golf course enterprise has many dimensions, including sports, technical operations, human resources, and the business dimension, which includes both marketing and financial management. The sports dimension covers the game itself and the enjoyment felt by golfers. This is the major purpose of the golf course. Without the players there is no need for the course, nor for the course superintendent. The technical operations dimension involves maintaining the golf course and keeping playing conditions desirable. This includes—but is not limited to—controlling weeds, cutting grass, and eliminating pests. The human resources dimension involves interactions among staff—including management and their staffs—and golf course employees and golfers. The business dimension involves, among many other things, acquiring resources, promoting the course and its activities, and managing resources to provide benefits to owners, players, employees, and the community.

Moreover, we can break down the business aspect of a golf course enterprise into further dimensions. For example, marketing activities involve promoting the course's benefits to current and potential players. Financial management involves planning and controlling the financial side of the enterprise, including its revenues, costs, and capital structure.

This book outlines the financial management dimensions of golf course management.

PURPOSE OF FINANCIAL MANAGEMENT

Financial management includes the two major dimensions of accounting and finance. We will define each to provide greater understanding; however, throughout this book we will make no differentiation between accounting and finance subtopics.

Accounting is defined as the process of identifying, measuring, and communicating economic information. Various tasks conducted by accountants include processing payroll, preparing the course's monthly and annual financial statements, and preparing tax returns.

Finance is defined as the process of obtaining, disbursing, and investing cash. Various tasks deal with monitoring cash balances, investing excess cash, and raising cash for capital projects through selling stock and/or borrowing funds.

Corporate offices of large hospitality firms often have separate accounting and finance departments; however, at the retail level—that is, where the operations take place—the accounting and finance activities are almost always merged and managed by a financial executive. The golf course level is our concern here, so further discussion will focus on financial management activities at the retail level.

Financial management at the golf course level is the process of managing the income and money flows associated with the business side of the course. The purposes are to ensure that the manager has sufficient funds available as needed, that the funds are used to acquire the proper resources, and that they are maintained at a proper level. Another element of financial management is economic efficiency and productivity, which is necessary to ensure that golf course operations are conducted with a minimum waste of resources.

Financial management is differentiated from other management topics, such as human resources management or turf management. However, it is clear that decisions made in these other areas will affect financial management. For example, if too much is spent on personnel, less money is available for other items, and this impact is shown on the course's financial statements.

The golf course superintendent must recognize the importance of financial management and its interrelationship with other dimensions of the course. The busy superintendent cannot afford to let decisions about physical condition of the course totally override the concern for financial management. For instance, golfers see the quality of turf and playing conditions every time they play a round, and may pressure the superintendent to improve conditions without concern for the costs involved. The superintendent makes observations and decisions daily and even hourly that affect the physical conditions of play.

Further, most golfers never see the financial condition of the club, except perhaps as it affects the level of their dues, assessments, and green fees. The superintendent will assist in preparing a budget once a year, and often thereafter may only look at the budget once a month. However, if ignored, extremely poor financial management can lead to an *involuntary career shift* for the superintendent who allows costs to consistently exceed the budget, who has excess inventory of some items and shortages of others, or who otherwise totally ignores financial management concerns—even if playing conditions are acceptable. Often, poor financial management, such as shortages of inventory items, will result in less than superb playing conditions.

FINANCIAL MANAGEMENT FOR DIFFERENT TYPES OF GOLF COURSES

Some elements of financial management are quite different in the various kinds of courses. Even though a superintendent might expect to work for a particular course or type of course for a long time, it is still important to understand the financial management of various kinds of courses. This will make career shifts easier, increase the opportunity to change courses, and improve the quality of communication about financial management—both on the job and at conferences, training programs, and seminars.

However, some elements of financial management are universal for all courses, such as efficiency, asset management, and economic decision making. Revenues and profitability vary in their application among private courses, semiprivate courses, and municipal courses. The three types will be discussed briefly.

The Private Golf Club

The private golf club is either a pure profit or a quasi-profit enterprise designed to meet the specific needs of club members. In a pure profit club, a person (or group of people) owns the facility and leases the facility and appropriate services to dues-paying members. The owner(s) may be a sole proprietorship, a partnership, or—most likely—a corporation. The major objective of the golf course enterprise is to provide a profit for the owner(s).

Financial management is performed in essentially the same way as it is done in any other business enterprise. The owner is responsible for club operations, which are often managed by hired professionals. If members are not satisfied with the club and do not renew their memberships, the owner(s) may suffer losses. If finances are not managed properly, the owner(s) will suffer a loss.

The quasi-profit club is owned by a group of persons who are also club members. These members purchase shares of ownership in the club. They also may be charged periodic dues (often monthly) and special assessments. Members elect a board of directors, which makes decisions affecting club policies and operations. The board is accountable to the club members.

Operations of the private golf club are described in the income statements and supporting schedules. The income statement (described in the next chapter) is a formal report that provides the following information:

1. Operational accountability of department managers, such as the golf course superintendent. For example, what were the payroll expenses for the month?
2. Revenue and expense subclassifications. What was the budget for revenues and expenses for the month? What was the difference between the budgeted and actual revenues and expenses?
3. How much profit was generated during the accounting period? Is the profit sufficient?

The *balance sheet* of a private golf club (discussed in greater detail in the next chapter) reflects the items owned (called *assets*) and amounts owed (called *liabilities*) by the club. Many questions can be answered with the balance sheet, including the following:

1. *Amount of cash on hand.* Is it sufficient to pay the club's current bills?
2. *Total assets and liabilities of the club.* How do the total assets compare to the total liabilities?
3. *Net worth of the club.* How much do the owners have invested in the club, and what is the net worth of the club?

Each of these questions is directly and indirectly affected by the decisions made by the golf course superintendent and other managers of the club.

The Semi-Private, Daily-Fee Course

Daily-fee courses are open to the public. The courses are operated strictly as a business venture, and are owned by an individual, partnership, or corporation. The operating policies are designed to yield a profit to the owner(s), as with any other kind of business. Some courses offer membership privileges as well. Because the superintendent's decisions will have a direct impact on the level of profit or loss of the course, much attention is paid to the quality of those decisions.

The objectives of financial reporting for semiprivate courses are similar to those shown above for the private golf club. The financial statements used by the semi-private golf club are the same.

The Municipal Golf Course

Municipal golf courses are constructed and operated by a tax-supported agency of government entity, such as a town, city, county, or recreational district. The major objective of the golf course operation is to provide golfing facilities to citizens at a minimal cost, rather than to make a profit. Within the governmental entity, the municipal golf course is typically part of a Parks and Recreation or similar department. Golf courses of this type are typically operated as an *enterprise fund*. That is, revenues and fees (not profit) of the course are expected to cover all costs of the course; thus, the course sustains itself by its own operations.

Municipal golf course operations are only partially self-supporting because revenues generated by green fees, snack bar sales, pro shop sales, and rentals are less than total costs. They are generally given financial support by the governmental unit from its tax revenues. This condition is often an unpopular one with governmental authorities and the taxpayers, so the burden is on golf course managers to be as efficient as possible in their financial management. Increasingly so, municipal courses are considering the profit potential as courses are being upgraded, or even with the development of new courses.

If the golf course generates a surplus of funds, the surplus can be returned to the municipality. This may occur because fees are set higher than necessary, because needed capital improvements are not made, or because operations are conducted on a bare-bones budget. Each of these conditions is unfavorable to the golfer.

Financial reporting for such municipal enterprises is similar to that of the profit-oriented golf course. The reports themselves are included as a part of the budget of the public entity sponsoring the course, and are reviewed periodically as a part of a formal budgeting process. The expected costs of providing user services are matched against expected revenues received from users to determine the amount to be budgeted for the activity in the next accounting period. Statements should be organized to highlight the costs of providing services, rather than just the bottom-line results. They will also show the extent of nonoperating inflows from appropriations from the governmental unit.

THE SUPERINTENDENT'S ROLE IN FINANCIAL MANAGEMENT

The golf course superintendent is a key decision maker in the financial management of any golf course. That is, practically all decisions made by the superintendent will be reflected, directly or indirectly, in the financial statements of the course. The quality of the superintendent's decisions will determine how efficiently the operations are conducted. Further, the quality of the superintendent' s operational decisions can be determined by careful analysis of the financial statements, as well as by the more direct observation of the physical condition of the course. Superintendents often report to a board, and their overall performance is evaluated by looking at the financial records and at the physical playing conditions of the golf course.

Superintendents must have sufficient authority to make decisions impacting the course for which they are responsible. This authority covers personnel matters and operational areas. Personnel matters include—but are not limited to—the hiring and dismissal of personnel. Operations include all the nonpersonnel matters, such as obtaining and using various supplies in order to maintain the golf course.

The golf course superintendent should view the accounting department as a supporter. The major purpose of the accounting department is to provide services such as writing paychecks, preparing monthly financial statements, and paying suppliers. Superintendents should feel at ease in directing questions of a financial nature to the accounting department, which maintains the accounting records. The accounting department should be able to answer questions such as these quickly and easily:

1. What was the cost of the fairway mower, and by what amount has it been depreciated?
2. What was the cost per gallon of Roundup purchased last July from XYZ company?
3. What is the average number of hours per week that the three maintenance employees have worked for the second quarter?

The chief accounting officer can also be helpful with the nonroutine type of questions, such as, "How is a discounted cash flow projection calculated?" Again, the accounting staff exists to help the superintendent in the area of financial management.

Centers of managerial authority and responsibility can be identified within a golf course operation or any enterprise. The authority and responsibilities of people in charge of the centers normally are specified on an organization chart and in job descriptions. In the most general way, different basic kinds of financial authority and responsibilities can be identified. Three types of financial responsibility centers follow:

1. *Profit center.* This is an organizational unit whose manager is responsible for generating profit from the unit. The manager of a profit center must be able to make decisions that will affect the amounts of both revenues and expenses at the same time. Thus, given the responsibility for managing a golf cart rental or a restaurant operation, the manager will make some decisions that will increase revenues and other decisions that will affect costs. These two types of decisions interact with each other to generate either a profit or a loss for the unit.

2. *Service center.* This is an organizational unit that is a user of funds, because it is designed to produce services for other departments. Funds are allocated by a budget to the unit to produce the desired result, since the operation itself does not generate its own revenues. The accounting department of the golf course enterprise is an example of a service center.

3. *Cost centers.* This is also an organizational unit that is a user of funds. Since it produces certain results, such as maintenance of the golf course, and does not generate its own funds, it is allocated funds through the budget process. Most golf course superintendents are managers of cost centers rather than profit centers. Cost and service centers are similar in that neither generates revenues directly. Cost centers differ from service centers, as service centers generally provide services to profit, service, and cost centers, while cost centers generally provide results for a single department.

Most of a superintendent's decisions result in expenses for the golf course enterprise. Examples include expenditures for water, fertilizer, and labor, as well as decisions that involve the purchase of equipment and the use and maintenance of the equipment. The outcome of these and other cost-generating decisions are visibly seen as improved playing conditions. The decisions of the superintendent will directly impact the financial health of the course, since they generate expenses that impact the profitability of the course.

In general, the superintendent's job is viewed as managing a cost center—course construction and maintenance is the objective to be reached, and funds are budgeted to accomplish this objective. In turn, the superintendent may also create cost centers that report to him/her, such as a repair center for maintaining equipment. Thus, the superintendent will prepare a budget that proposes a level of course construction and maintenance for the coming year, makes operating decisions about what will consume funds, and will be reviewed at year's end.

Since the golf course is often the major activity of golfing enterprises, the superintendent's role is critical to the success of the operation.

Although the superintendent might not be directly involved with revenues, failure will generally lead to a declining quality in the golf course and might eventually lead to financial failure of the enterprise. When the course is maintained in excellent condition, revenues are increased by the number of rounds, golf cart revenues, pro shop sales, food and beverage sales, and so on. Thus, one cannot overly stress the key role of the superintendent in the financial success of the golfing enterprise.

The increasing costs of maintaining golf courses for private country clubs are shown in Exhibit 1.1. In 1983, the average annual costs to maintain a hole were $16,000. Twenty years later, this annual cost had surpassed $75,000 based on PKF Worldwide's latest survey.[1]

Brief Overview of the Golf Industry [2]

According to the National Golf Foundation, there were 25.8 million golfers over the age of 12 in the United States in 2003. Female golfers made up 24 percent of the golfing public.

There are more than 15,800 golf courses in the United States, of which 73 percent are open to the public. This is a 18.5 percent increase since 1986 (13,353 to 15,827 courses). In 2002, 220 new golf courses were opened. At the end of 2002, there were 408 courses under construction and an additional 376 are in the planning stage.

---

[1] PKF International, *Clubs in Town & Country, 2003* (Fairfax,VA: PKF International, 2003).

[2] National Golf Foundation (www.ngf.org).

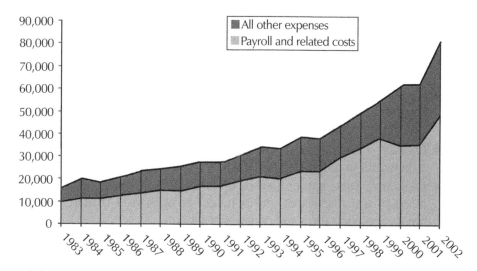

Exhibit 1.1. Twenty-Year History of Golf Costs per Hole.
Source: PKF International, *Clubs in Town & Country, 2003* (Fairfax, VA: PKF International, 2003)

Golfers spent $23.5 billion on equipment, fees, and dues in 2001. Just over 74 percent of all spending was for green fees and dues. The average 18-hole daily-fee course has 30,000 rounds of golf played per year and employs 13 full-time people, while the average 9-hole daily-fee course has 17,000 rounds played each year and employs 4 people.

The median total annual revenue and gross revenue per round of golf by type of course for 2000 was as follows:

	Median Total Revenue	Gross Revenue per Round
Municipal	$1,069,000	$25
Daily Fee	992,000	32
Private	2,391,000	95

OUTLINE OF CHAPTERS 2 THROUGH 9

The remainder of the text will be organized around the following topics:

◆ *Chapter 2.* Financial statements for golf course activities are discussed. The two major statements—the income statement and the balance sheet—will be explained. It is important to know what is included on each statement and how they interrelate.

◆ *Chapter 3.* This chapter includes a discussion of records and procedures. Accounting for inventory, equipment, and payroll is covered.

◆ *Chapter 4.* This chapter includes the golf course operating statement. The details of the statement are presented, as well as operational analysis of this statement.

◆ *Chapter 5.* This chapter presents techniques for analyzing financial statements to determine the financial success of a golf course.

◆ *Chapter 6.* This chapter focuses on breakeven analysis. Various types of costs are discussed, and a model is presented to determine a breakeven point for a golf course operation.

◆ *Chapter 7.* This chapter is used to discuss operating budgets. The budget process, budget preparation techniques, and budgetary control procedures are presented.

◆ *Chapter 8.* This chapter discusses capital investment budgeting. Methods of analyzing purchase decisions, repair/replace, and other nonroutine decisions are presented.

◆ *Chapter 9.* This chapter presents leasing. Advantages and disadvantages of leases are discussed, as well as the lease versus buy decision process.

SUMMARY

Sound financial management is a basic requirement for the success of a golf course enterprise, whether it is private or public. The quality of a superintendent's decisions will directly affect the financial well-being of any of the various kinds of courses. The financial health of a course is shown directly in financial statements that summarize the financial activities of the course. The quality of a superintendent's decisions can be determined, in part, by analysis of financial statements.

Overview of Financial Statements

A major objective of financial management is the communication of financial information. This is typically accomplished by using various reports and financial statements. A daily report of operations for a golf course enterprise would generally include the number of rounds of golf played, the amount of daily green fees, and similar statistics for other operations of the enterprise. The financial statements are generally prepared monthly and on an annual basis. The major financial statements prepared monthly include the *Income Statement* and the *Balance Sheet*. These two statements will be discussed in this chapter. Other financial statements include the *Statement of Cash Flows* and the *Statement of Retained Earnings* (for golf course enterprises organized as corporations).

The financial statements are generally prepared by the accounting department of the golf course enterprise. Although most information is based on the accounting records processed by the accounting department, the golf course superintendent is involved with various documents to support these basic records. For example, most superintendents approve the time cards for hourly employees that serve as the basis for payroll checks, and superintendents specify the account classification for golf course expenses.

The superintendent is a user of financial information and ideally will receive copies of the monthly financial statements. Some golf course enterprises choose to provide their superintendents with only the golf course operations portion of the income statement. However, in order to increase their awareness of the role and position of the golf course as part of the entire operation, it is highly desirable that superintendents receive a full set of the monthly financial statements.

The operation's budget numbers for each month are generally included on the monthly income statement and accompanying schedules so that the superintendent can easily compare the operating results to the budgeted numbers for the accounting period. Significant differences between the budget and actuals should be analyzed with the purpose of determining the causes of the differences and taking corrective action. In addition, the monthly financial statements include the year-to-date numbers, which show how the operation is performing from the beginning of the course's fiscal year through the most recent month.

By comparing this month's numbers to prior months, the golf course superintendent can detect trends and potential problem areas that require action. In addition, the superintendent can compare this month's numbers (or numbers for other time periods) with industry averages. This comparison is also useful for spotting potential weaknesses. For example, PKF International produces an annual report of club statistics that some superintendents find useful for comparative purposes. However, industry statistics are simply averages and should not be construed to be standards.

THE INCOME STATEMENT

The income statement summarizes the results of operations of a golf course enterprise for a period of time. Many not-for-profit clubs refer to this statement as the *Statement of Activities* in their financial statements prepared for members and outside users. Municipal units often refer to this statement as the *Statement of Revenues and Expenses.* The income statement shows both revenues and expenses for a period of time, and the difference between the two is called *net income.* When expenses exceed revenues during the accounting period, the difference is a net loss. Although income statements generally include the budgeted amounts for the accounting period and year-to-date numbers, to simplify the illustrations used in this chapter, monthly income statements will include only amounts for the month.

Exhibit 2.1 contains the income statement for the hypothetical Sample Golf Club. The presentation is for illustrative purposes only, and is simplified (as only a few selected revenues and expenses are shown). The format shown in Exhibit 2.1 would be used by private, semiprivate, and municipal golf courses. Each element of the hypothetical income statement will be briefly discussed.

Revenues		
Green fees		$60,000
Cart rentals		20,000
Total		80,000
Expenses		
Salaries and wages	$32,000	
Payroll taxes and benefits	8,000	
Operating supplies	10,000	
Repairs	5,000	
Energy costs	8,000	
Depreciation	5,000	
Other expenses	7,000	75,000
Net income		$ 5,000

EXHIBIT 2.1. Sample Golf Club Income Statement for the month of June 20X1

Revenue

The revenue items reflect the sources of funds earned by the enterprise. Revenue is sometimes referred to as *sales* and *income*. For the Sample Golf Club, revenues include green fees paid by the golfers, plus the charges to the golfers for renting carts. We will assume that the Sample Golf Club only accepts cash payment for green fees and cart rentals, so $80,000 in cash was received during the month of June. Other types of revenues that golf course businesses earn include dues, special assessments, initiation fees, sales for various products sold, and interest income.

Revenue is recorded when earned by the golf course. In some cases, the revenue is earned and the golfer pays cash at the same time, while in other situations revenue is earned and is recorded, but the golfer pays in the following month. For accounting purposes, revenue is recorded when earned, regardless of when the cash is received. Since most golf course superintendents manage a cost center, their decisions generally have only an indirect impact on revenues.

Expenses

Expenses, sometimes referred to as *costs*, are the use of the enterprise's resources to generate sales. Expenses of the hypothetical Sample Golf Club include salaries and wages, payroll taxes and benefits, operating supplies, repairs, energy costs, depreciation expense, and other expenses. Expenses not shown in Exhibit 2.1 that are incurred by golf courses might also include rent, interest, property taxes, income taxes, and cost of goods sold, just to mention a few.

Salaries and Wages include the amount of salaries and wages *earned* by employees of the course for the accounting period. The key word is *earned*, because how much the employees were paid this month is not the question, but rather, how much they earned. Wages Earned but not paid during the month are accrued at the end of the month and paid in the following month. The accrual process will be discussed in the following chapter.

Payroll Taxes and Benefits include taxes on employee salaries and wages. The major payroll tax is FICA. FICA tax is withheld from each employee's check, matched by the employer (the golf course enterprise), and then paid to the U.S. Treasury. The matched portion is the expense to the golf course. (Payroll taxes will be discussed in more detail in Chapter 3.) Benefits vary by business but include the cost of health insurance and other employee benefits. Operating Supplies would include all the various supplies used by the Sample Golf Club. Fertilizers, chemicals, and office supplies are some examples. For illustrative purposes, these were included in a single line to simplify the presentation; however, in reality the statement should be sufficiently detailed to allow the superintendent to effectively manage the costs of the golf course. The superintendent may desire to have supplies broken down into five or six major categories to provide a clear understanding of the detail of this expense area.

Supplies should be expensed as used, rather than when purchased, when the amounts are significant. To accomplish this, supplies are often inventoried. The process of inventorying and subsequently expensing supplies will be presented in later chapters of this book.

Repairs includes all the repairs of equipment and other assets. For example, the cost of parts to repair a mower would be shown on this line of the income statement. Repairs to buildings, office equipment, furniture, and so on are also shown as repairs. Energy costs include the costs of water, electricity, natural gas, and other fuels. Separate accounts are often maintained for each type of resource in order to allow closer management of these costs.

Depreciation expense results from writing off a portion of the cost of property and equipment to expense. For the Sample Golf Club, depreciation expense for the month is $5,000. The concept and processes related to depreciation will be presented in further detail in the next chapter.

Finally, our hypothetical enterprise shows *Other Expenses* on its income statement. This line item is used for expenses not classified in other categories. In practice, it is desirable that this line be relatively small because it reflects expenses not specifically classified and does not lend itself to as tight a management as do costs that are classified.

Some general comments regarding expense classifications are warranted at this point. It is extremely helpful to categorize expenses into classifications to assist in managerial analysis of operations. Some golf courses may have a very general classification of expenses—perhaps only six to eight categories, including a relatively large "other expenses" category—preventing detailed cost analysis. Other golf course accounting systems may have a very extensive classification, with expenses assigned to various activities and to various responsibility centers, allowing detailed cost analysis.

The account titles are usually set up by an accountant who initially designs the accounting system. The accounts are listed in a *chart of accounts*. If the chart of accounts does not provide for detailed accounting desired by the superintendent, the superintendent should request that additional accounts be included. Remember that the accounting department is a service department, with the purpose of providing accounting services to users of accounting information. In addition, the superintendent often determines which account a particular transaction should be entered into. For example, the travel expenses associated with a business trip might be associated with either a training expense or a buying trip. If the chart of accounts has accounts for various kinds of travel, it will be necessary for the superintendent to indicate which account is applicable. Therefore, the superintendent's daily operating decisions will affect the amounts recorded in the expense accounts.

In addition, the superintendents must be consistent in their specification of account classifications. For example, an expenditure for equipment repairs should always be recorded as *repairs* rather than the "careless" recording of this type of expenditure as a repair most of the time but on occasion as supplies.

Net Income

Net income—the *bottom line* on the income statement—is the profit of the club for the period. It is the difference between revenue and expenses. For the Sample Golf Club, net income is $5,000 for June 20X1.

It is important not to confuse the terms *income, revenue,* and *cash.* *Income* is a measure of profitability. *Revenue* results from sales of goods or services. *Cash* is funds in the form of money. Profit may or may not be in the form of cash, and revenue may or may not result in an immediate increase in cash.

Accounting for golf course operations is based on accrual accounting. In fairly simple terms, this means that revenue is recognized when earned and expenses are recognized when incurred. This differs considerably from cash-based accounting, which recognizes revenue when cash is received from golfers for services provided and recognizes expenses when cash is paid for goods and/or services received. Cash accounting is acceptable only for the very smallest of business enterprises. The concept of cash versus accrual accounting will be discussed in greater detail in the next chapter.

THE BALANCE SHEET

The balance sheet of a golf course enterprise shows assets, liabilities, and owners' equity. The balance sheet, sometimes referred to as the *Statement of Financial Position,* is prepared as of the last day of the accounting period—that is, the last day of the month for monthly financial statements, and the last day of the year for the annual financials.

The balance sheet—by reflecting the amount of assets, the debts of the enterprise, and the net worth of the owners—reflects the *accounting equation* as follows:

Assets = Liabilities + Owners' Equity

The first claims to the assets are by creditors, and are referred to as liabilities. The residual claims are by owners; thus, the accounting equation can be reconfigured to reflect that claims of the owners are as follows:

Assets – Liabilities = Owners' Equity

The balance sheets used by private and semiprivate golf clubs are classified by major categories of assets and liabilities. The major classifications of assets are current, property and equipment, and other. The major classifications of liabilities are current and long-term. These classifications are reflected in the balance sheet of our hypothetical Sample Golf Club in Exhibit 2.2.

A quick review of the Sample Golf Club's balance sheet reveals that the statement balances—that is, assets of $940,000—are equal to liabilities and owners' equity of $940,000.

Assets		
Current Assets		
Cash		$ 10,000
Inventories		15,000
Total current assets		25,000
Property and Equipment		
Land	$200,000	
Building	500,000	
Equipment	300,000	
Less: accumulated depreciation	(100,000)	900,000
Other Assets		15,000
Total Assets		$940,000
Liabilities and Equity		
Current Liabilities		
Accounts payable		$ 15,000
Wages payable		3,000
Total current liabilities		18,000
Long-Term Debt		
Mortgage payable		502,000
Notes payable		150,000
Total current liabilities		652,000
Total Liabilities		670,000
Owners' Equity		
Capital stock		100,000
Retained earnings		170,000
Total owners' equity		270,000
Total Liabilities and Owners' Equity		$940,000

EXHIBIT 2.2. Sample Golf Club Balance Sheet, June 30, 20X1

Assets

The major categories of assets are current, property and equipment, and other. *Current assets* consist only of cash and inventories. Current assets are listed in order of their liquidity—that is, how quickly they can be converted to cash or used in the business. Current assets not shown in Exhibit

2.2 that golf course enterprises might have include Temporary Investments, Accounts Receivable, Notes Receivable, and Prepaid Expenses. In order for an item to be classified as a current asset, it must be cash, must be converted to cash, or must be used in operations within a year from the balance sheet date.

The second category of assets of our hypothetical golf enterprise is *Property and Equipment*. The three assets listed are land, building, and equipment. These assets are listed at their cost to the enterprise. Depreciation related to the equipment is subtracted to determine net property and equipment. The accounting department of the enterprise maintains detailed records for each piece of property and equipment that show the date the item was purchased, cost, and depreciation for each year. The accounting records show the net book value for each item—that is, its cost less its associated depreciation, which may differ widely from the market value of the item. For example, a mower might have cost $30,000 three years ago, and it has been depreciated over the three years by $18,000. The net book value today is the cost of the mower ($30,000) less the accumulated depreciation of $18,000, which is equal to $12,000. The market value today of the mower is what the mower is worth—that is, how much it would cost to replace it in its current condition. The market value of the mower was equal to its book value at the date of purchase. However, after that point, the market value of the mower may be higher or lower than the net book value of the mower. Generally, buildings and equipment of an enterprise are accounted for at their cost, less accumulated depreciation. At various times throughout the life of the asset, the market value may exceed the net book value of the item; however, the accounts are not adjusted to reflect a higher market value, but the accountant continues to account for the item based on its original cost. The superintendent most likely would have a reasonable idea what the item's market value is, and he/she would use this additional information in the decision making processes.

The final category of assets of the Sample Golf Club is *other*. These are assets other than current assets and property and equipment. In this case, "other" assets are the amounts deposited with utility companies in order to receive their services. If in the future this enterprise discontinues the use of their services, the deposits will be refunded.

Other categories of assets of golf course enterprises include Investments and *Noncurrent Receivables*. Investments would include the cost of land for future development and other long-term investments of the course's cash. Noncurrent receivables are notes receivable that are not due to be paid to the enterprise within twelve months from the balance sheet date.

Liabilities

Liabilities of an enterprise represent the future obligations at the balance sheet. Obligations due within one year are classified as current liabilities. For the Sample Golf Club, only the accounts for Accounts Payable and Wages Payable are shown. *Accounts payable* represents amounts due to vendors for supplies and services received but not paid for as of the balance sheet date. *Wages payable* is the total of unpaid wages as of the balance sheet date. In general, other current liabilities would include notes payable, taxes payable, accrued expenses payable and the current maturities of long-term debt. The long-term debt of the hypothetical golf course includes mortgage payable and the current maturities of long-term debt.

For both of these line items, the amounts shown are not due within twelve months of the balance sheet date. When a portion of long-term debt becomes due within twelve months, the amount due is reclassified as a current liability.

Generally, decisions by golf course superintendents have little impact on liability accounts. Decisions by the course's financial executive, such as the borrowing of funds on a long-term basis to finance the purchase of equipment used to maintain the golf course, does impact the liabilities of the enterprise.

Owners' Equity

The Owners' Equity category shown on the balance sheet reflects the claims of owners on the assets of the business. As shown previously, assets minus liabilities equals owners' equity.

The Sample Golf Club was organized as a corporation, and the simplified owners' equity section reflects the two accounts *Capital Stock* and *Retained Earnings*. In general, the Owners' Equity section on the balance sheet differs with the form of ownership of the golf course:

1. In a sole proprietorship, equity is the difference between assets (owned by the proprietor) and liabilities (owed by the proprietor). The firm's books will include an account showing the owners' capital, such as J. Doe, Capital. Funds withdrawn by the owner from the enterprise are taken from this account. These withdrawals are reductions of capital and are not regarded as salary to the owner.
2. In a partnership, each partner will have a Capital account, reflecting the partner's ownership share. The beginning balance is the

partner's original capital contribution. As the partnership earns profits, a proportionate share is recorded in the Capital account of each partner. Partners then make withdrawals from their partner accounts.

3. In a corporation, equity is recorded in shareholder accounts. Initially, the account balance reflects the par, or stated, value of the stock issued and then *Additional Paid-in Capital* to reflect owner contribution in excess of the par amount. For example, assume the original stockholders paid $40 per share to the corporation for 50,000 shares of $20 par value stock. The balance sheet would show Capital Stock of $1,000,000 (50,000 shares times $20 par value) and Additional Paid-in Capital of $1,000,000 (50,000 shares times the excess of $40 over the par value of $20). As the corporation earns net income, it is transferred to the Retained Earnings account. Income is distributed to owners by paying dividends out of the Retained Earnings account.

4. In a municipal golf course owned and operated by a governmental unit, the Equity accounts are replaced by a Fund Balance account. The fund balance shows the amount of capital transferred by the governmental unit and the amount of earnings by the golf course after expenses are deducted from gross revenues.

The Retained Earnings account reflects simply the earnings retained by the enterprise. The profit of an enterprise for a period of time is shown on the income statement. At the end of the accounting period (generally annually) the profit is transferred from the income statement to the retained earnings account on the balance sheet. Dividends paid to the owners reduce retained earnings. Thus, the balance in retained earnings is a net result of all profits earned by the golf enterprise and dividends paid to owners.

UNIFORM SYSTEMS OF ACCOUNTS

The National Golf Course Owners Association (NGCOA) and the Club Managers Association of America (CMAA) have each developed their own uniform system of accounts. The CMAA's uniform system addresses accounting for private country clubs while NGCOA's uniform system covers accounting for public and resort golf courses.

The major purpose in using a uniform system of accounts is that it provides for standardized accounting. The format of financial statements provided in a uniform system can be easily adapted by a specific course operation. A specific enterprise may want to have more expense accounts related to the operation than are encompassed in the uniform system's financial statements, so the system must be adapted to meet the needs of the specific golf course operation. Exhibits 2.3 and 2.4 are recommended formats of the balance sheet and income statement taken from the NGCOA's uniform system of accounts. You will notice that there is considerably more detail than shown in the illustrations used in this chapter. Each golf course must adapt the proposed statements to suit its needs.

In Exhibit 2.4 there is a column titled *schedules* that refers to several accompanying schedules for responsibility centers. Schedule 1 is for golf course operations of the business. Schedule 2 is for the cart rental activities of the course, while schedule 3 is used for the pro shop. Schedules 1 through 9 reflect both revenues and expenses.Schedule 10 is used for reporting the detail of other income. The remaining schedules (11–19) are used to report overhead expenses of the business.

Real World Financial Statements

The appendix to this chapter contains the Annual Report of the Detroit Golf Club (DGC) ended August 31 of 1999 and 2000. The financial statements for the two years included in the annual report are as follows:

◆ Statement of Operations and Changes in Member's Equity
◆ Balance sheets
◆ Statement of Cash Flows

The financial statements, especially the statement of operations, are summarized; no detailed schedules are provided because the annual report is provided primarily for members and outside users such as lenders. Most likely, the monthly financial statements provided to the club's general manager and other management members (including the golf course superintendent) include numerous supplementary schedules covering operations.

In addition, the notes to the financial statements and the report by the independent auditor are included in DGC's annual report. In order to gain a reasonable understanding of the financial statements, the notes to the financial statements and the auditors' report should be carefully read.

	Date	
	20	**20**
Current Assets		
Cash and cash equivalents	$_____	$_____
Marketable securities	_____	_____
Receivables		
Accounts receivable		
Notes receivable		
Other		
Total	_____	_____
Less allowance for doubtful accounts	_____	_____
and notes		
Inventories		
Golf shop		
Food		
Beverage	_____	_____
	_____	_____
Prepaid Expenses		
Insurance		
Real estate taxes		
Golf course and other supplies		
Other	_____	_____
	_____	_____
Other current assets	_____	_____
Total current assets	_____	_____
Investments	_____	_____
Property and Equipment		
Land and land improvements		
Buildings and building improvements		
Furniture and equipment	_____	_____
Less accumulated depreciation and	_____	_____
Amortization		
Other Assets		
Deferred charges	_____	_____
Other	_____	_____
Total Assets	$_____	$_____

EXHIBIT 2.3. Balance Sheet: Assets

| | Date | |
	20__	**20__**
Current Liabilities	$_____	$_____
Notes payable (short-term)		
Current portion of long-term debt		
Accounts payable		
Taxes payable and accrued		
Payroll		
Sales		
Income		
Accrued liabilities		
Salaries and wages		
Interest		
Professional fees		
Unearned income		
Other current liabilities	_____	_____
Total current liabilities	_____	_____
Long-Term Liabilities		
Notes payable		
Mortgage payable	_____	_____
Total long-term liabilities	_____	_____
Less portion due within one year	_____	_____
Deferred Income Taxes	_____	_____
Stockholders' Equity/Enterprise Fund		
Capital stock or equity	_____	_____
Paid-in capital	_____	_____
Retained earnings/enterprise fund		
Balance, beginning of year		
Net income for the year	_____	_____
Balance, end of year	_____	_____
Total stockholders' equity/enterprise Fund	_____	_____
	$_____	$_____

EXHIBIT 2.3 (*cont'd*). Balance Sheet: Liabilities and Stockholders' Equity/Enterprise Fund

	Schedules	Period Ending	
		20	**20**
Departmental and Sports Income			
Golf course operations	1	$	$
Cart rentals	2		
Pro shop	3		
Other sports activities	4-6		
Food and beverage	7		
Lockers	8		
Other operated departments	9	____	____
Other income	10	____	____
Total income			
Departmental and Sports Costs and Expenses			
Golf course operations	1		
Cart rentals	2		
Pro shop	3		
Other sports activities	4-6		
Food and beverage	7		
Lockers	8		
Other operated departments	9		
Total costs and expenses		____	____
Income before undistributed operating expenses		____	____
Undistributed Operating Expenses			
Clubhouse expense	11		
Administrative and general	12		
Advertising and sales promotion	13		
Heat, light, and power	14		
Repairs and maintenance	15	____	____
Total undistributed operating expenses			
Gross operating profit before fixed charges		____	____
Fixed Charges			
Insurance-fire and general liability	16		
Rent and property taxes	17		
Interest expense		____	____
Total fixed charges		____	____

EXHIBIT 2.4. Statement of Income and Expense

	Schedules	Period Ending	
		20___	20___
Income before provision for depreciation		$_____	$_____
Provision for Depreciation	18	_____	_____
Income (loss) before income taxes			
	19		
Income Taxes			
Current		_____	_____
Deferred		_____	_____
Total income taxes		_____	_____
Net income (loss)		$_____	$_____

EXHIBIT 2.4 (*cont'd*). Statement of Income and Expense

SUMMARY

The two basic financial statements prepared on a monthly and annual basis are the income statement and the balance sheet. The income statement reflects the operations of the golf course by showing both revenues and expenses. The difference between revenues and expenses is profit for the golf course enterprise.

The balance sheet prepared as of the last day of the accounting period shows the assets, liabilities, and owners' equity of the enterprise. The statements reveal the book value of assets, the total amount owed by the enterprise, and the residual value of the assets belonging to the owner.

Uniform systems of accounts have been developed by various trade associations. These systems provide standardized reporting formats for the major financial statements.

APPENDIX: Detroit Golf Club Annual Report, Year Ended August 31, 2000

Statement of Operations and Changes in Members' Equity

| | Year Ended August 31 | | | | | |
| | 2000 | | | 1999 | | |
	Operating	Capital	Total	Operating	Capital	Total
Income						
Dues	$ 3,157,860	$ 312,593	$ 3,470,453	$ 3,029,081	$ 309,632	$ 3,338,713
Cafe and bar	2,757,725	-	2,757,725	2,415,548	-	2,415,548
Golf privileges	694,175	-	694,175	654,945	-	654,945
Golf carts	709,772	-	709,772	761,534	-	761,534
Golf service fee	195,555	-	195,555	366,547	-	366,547
Locker rental	101,608	-	101,608	66,294	-	66,294
Initiation and transfer fees	-	821,804	821,804	-	887,954	887,954
Proceeds from Inheritance	-	50,000	50,000	-	-	-
Proceeds of sale from art work	-	-	-	-	785,650	785,650
Interest and other income	78,889	145,713	224,602	79,660	133,683	213,343
Total income	7,695,584	1,330,110	9.025,694	7,373,609	2,116,919	9,490,528
Expenses						
Cafe and bar	2,588,502	-	2,588,502	2,402,443	-	2,402,443
Golf course and ground maintenance	1,614.239	-	1,614.239	1,532,267	-	1,532,267
Golf service operations	400,756	-	400,756	380,485	-	380,485
Golf cart maintenance	100,331	-	100,331	73,646	-	73,646
Main clubhouse	1,046,001	-	1,046,001	986,401	-	986,401
Locker rooms	189,190	-	189,190	166,707	-	166,707
Swimming and tennis	84,695	-	84,695	73,401	-	73,401
Caddie and other committees	348,255	-	348,255	334,176	-	334,176
General and administrative	1,501,994	-	1,501,994	1,411,939	-	1,411,939
Building	-	705,778	705,778	-	2,014,561	2,014,561
Equipment—main clubhouse	-	217,809	217,809	-	334,653	334,653
Furniture and fixtures	-	72,804	72,804	-	175,306	175,306
Greens equipment	-	167,909	167,909	-	144,023	144,023
Golf carts	-	115,198	115,198	-	3,281	3,281
Swimming pool	-	10,649	10,649	-	6,562	6,562
Golf course improvements	-	848,754	848,754	-	1,096,181	1,096,181
Paving—Cart, parking, service and other roads	-	7,840	7,840	-	10,252	10,252
Interest expense	-	211,036	211,036	-	93,228	93,228
Miscellaneous	-	4,801	4,801	-	45,864	45,864
Total expenses	7,873,983	2,362,578	10,236,541	7,361,465	3,923,911	11,285,376
Increase (Decrease) in Unappropriated Members' Equity—Before transfers	(178,379)	(1,032,468)	(1,210,647)	12,144	(1,806,992)	(1,794,848)
Net Transfers	178,379	(178,379)	-	(12,144)	12,144	-
Decrease in Unappropriated Members' Equity	-	(1,210,647)	(1,210,647)	-	(1,794,848)	(1,794,848)
Members' Equity—Beginning of year	-	1,310,567	1,310,567	-	3,105,415	3,105,415
Members' Equity—End of year	$ -	$ 99,720	$ 99,720	$ -	$ 1,310,567	$ 1,310,567

Detroit Golf Club Balance Sheet

	August 31	
	2000	1999
ASSETS		
Current Assets		
Cash and cash equivalents	$ 554,400	$ 788,837
Accounts receivable	1,171,208	1,145,964
Clubhouse restoration project—Notes receivable (Note 2)	201,275	447,726
Notes receivable (Note 1)	310,506	230,739
Inventories	118,974	105,688
Prepaid expenses	20,211	17,356
Total current assets	2,376,574	2,736,310
Clubhouse Restoration Project—Notes receivable (Note 2)	911,745	1,086,736
Cash and cash equivalents		
Notes receivable (Note 1)	254,517	284,478
Land, Buildings and Equipment	6,030,546	6,030,546
Total assets	$ 9,573,382	$ 10,138,070
LIABILITIES AND MEMBERS' EQUITY		
Current liabilities		
Accounts payable and accrued expenses	$ 383,695	$ 628,767
Accrued payroll and payroll taxes	213,182	268,161
Deferred revenue	224,343	87,181
Deferred transfer fees (Note 1)	310,506	230,739
Other accrued liabilities	305,342	122,857
Notes payable (Note 4)	1,580,534	500,541
Total current liabilities	3,017,602	1,838,246
Deferred transfer fees (Note 1)	254,517	284,478
Notes payable (Note 4)	1,942,543	2,126,779
Refundable deposits (Note 2)	4,259,000	4,578,000
Total liabilities	9,473,662	8,827,503
Members' Equity		
Members' stock—$2,191 average stated value Class A—Authorized, issued and outstanding—503 shares	1,102,110	1,102,110
Unappropriated (deficit)	(1,002,390)	208,457
Total members' equity	99,720	1,310,567
Total liabilities and members' equity	$ 9,573,382	$ 10,138,070

Detroit Golf Club Statement of Cash Flows

	Year Ended August 31	
	2000	1999
Cash Flows from Operating Activities		
Decrease in unappropriated members' equity	$ (1,210,847)	$ (1,794,848)
Adjustments to reconcile decrease in unappropriated members' equity to net cash from operating activities		
(Increase) decrease in assets		
Accounts receivable	(25,244)	81,930
Inventories and prepaid expenses	(16,141)	820
Increase (decrease) in liabilities		
Accounts payable and accrued expenses	(245,072)	6,130
Payroll and payroll taxes and other accrued liabilities	127,506	57,786
Deferred revenue	137,162	(134,317)
Net cash used in operating activities	(1,232,636)	(1,782,499)
Cash Flows from Financing Activities		
Collections on clubhouse restoration notes	286,742	562,318
Repayment of member deposits	(184,300)	(199,034)
Principal payments on notes payable	(154,243)	-
Proceeds from debt - Net of repayments	-	1,452,320
Deferred revenue	224,343	87,181
Net increase in line of credit	1,050,000	350,000
Net cash provided by financing activities	998,199	2,165,604
Net increase (Decrease) in Cash and Cash Equivalents	(234,437)	383,105
Cash and Cash Equivalents—Beginning of year	788,837	405,732
Cash and Cash Equivalents—End of year	$ 554,400	$ 788,837
Supplemental Cash Flow Information—Cash paid for interest	$ 211,036	$ 93,228

Detroit Golf Club, Notes to Financial Statements
August 31, 2000 and 1999

Note 1 – Significant Accounting Policies

Detroit Golf Club (the "Club") is a not-for-profit Michigan corporation organized to provide dining, golf and other recreational activities to its members. The Club's revenue is derived primarily from the collection of Club dues, food and beverage revenue, greens and cart fees and other social club charges. The Club members are located primarily in southeastern Michigan and accounts receivable are due primarily from those members.

Significant accounting policies of the Club include the following:

Cash Equivalents – Cash equivalents include investments in certificates of deposit with maturities of three months or less.

Inventories – Inventories are stated at the lower of cost (first-out method) or market.

Land, Buildings and Equipment – Land, buildings and equipment additions and improvements are generally expensed as incurred in the Capital Fund. In lieu of capitalizing additions and improvements and making annual provisions for depreciation on those assets, the Club allocates a portion of dues, initiation and transfer fees, assessments for capital improvements and net income (loss) from operations, to (from) the Capital Fund. The amount reported on the balance sheet for land, buildings and equipment represents the cost of the land of $264,851 the depreciated cost of other capitalized assets of $608,458 as of August 31, 1947 and the cost of the 1997–1998 clubhouse restoration project totaling $5,157,237 which was capitalized because of its extraordinary size. The effect of not capitalizing and depreciating all land, buildings and equipment which is required by generally accepted accounting principles is not practicably determinable.

Transfer Fees – Certain members have the option of deferring payment of a portion of the stock transfer fee. These amounts are represented by notes receivable due over a period of three years. Revenue from the transfer fee is recognized in the Capital Fund over the deferral period.

Use of Estimates – The preparation of financial statements in conformity with generally accepted accounting principles requires management to make estimates and assumptions that affect the reported amounts of assets and liabilities and disclosure of contingent assets and liabilities at the date of the financial statements and the reported amounts of revenue and expenses during the reporting period. Actual results could differ from those estimates.

Functional Expense Classification – The Club's expenses are comprised of $1,501,994 and $1,411,939 for administration and $8,736,547 and $9,873,437 for operations for the years ended August 31,2000 and 1999, respectively.

Note 2 – Clubhouse Restoration Project

In December 1995, the members approved a proposal to make significant renovations and improvements to the clubhouse. As of August 31, 1998, the Club completed these renovations. The project was financed from the proceeds of noninterest-bearing deposits made by the members. The deposits are due over a period of up to 10 years and, upon departure, are refundable, partially refundable or nonrefundable to members determined by membership approval data. The expected cash inflows from these uncollected deposits for the years ending August 31 are as follows:

2001	$ 201,275
2002	185,642
2003	192,146
2004	204,108
2005	194,676
Thereafter	135,173
Total	$1,113,020

Note 3 – Pension Plans

The Club has three pension plans covering substantially all employees. Costs under defined contribution multiemployer plans for union employees are based on time worked and amounted to $71,417 and $57,730 in 2000 and 1999, respectively.

Costs under the Club's 401(k) plan are based on a percentage of the participants' compensation and approximated $97,000 and$95,000 in 2000 and 1999, respectively.

Note 4 – Notes Payable

Notes payable consist of the following:

	2000	1999
$2,000,000 Unsecured revolving line of credit with interest on outstanding borrowings payable at the bank's prevailing prime rate minus 1.00 percent (8.5 percent at August 31,2000)	$1,400,000	$ 350,000
Note payable, unsecured, bearing interest at 7.25 percent due in monthly installments of $17,692 including interest, with any remaining balance due in 2009	1,406,791	1,500,000
Note payable, unsecured, bearing interest of 7.25 percent due in monthly installments of $9,686 including interest, with any remaining balance due in 2008	716,286	777,320
Total	3,523,077	2,627,320
Less current portion	1,580,534	500,541
Long-term portion	$1,942,543	$2,126,779

Minimum future principal payments on long-term debt are as follows:

Years Ending August 31	Amount
2001	$1,580,534
2001	194,003
2003	208,541
2004	224,167
2005	240,965
and thereafter	1,074,867
Total	$3,523,077

Note 5 – Federal Income Taxes

The Club is a non-profit corporation exempt from federal income taxes under Section 501(c)(7) of the Internal Revenue Code of 1986, as amended. The Club is, however, subject to tax on its unrelated business income, for which provision has been made in the accompanying financial statements.

Independent Auditor's Report

To the Board of Directors
Detroit Golf Club

We have audited the accompanying balance sheet of the Detroit Golf Club as of August 31, 2000 and 1999 and the related statements of operations and changes in members' equity and cash flows for the years then ended. These financial statements are the responsibility of the club's Board of Directors and management. Our responsibility is to express an opinion on the financial statements based on our audits.

We conducted our audits in accordance with generally accepted auditing standards. Those standards require that we plan and perform the audits to obtain reasonable assurance about whether the financial statements are free of material misstatement. An audit includes examining, on a test basis, evidence supporting the amounts and overall financial statement presentation. We believe that our audits provide a reasonable basis for our opinion.

As described in Note 1 to the financial statements, the Club does not generally capitalize buildings and equipment or provide for depreciation on those assets. Generally accepted accounting principles require the capitalization and depreciation of such items. The effect on the financial statements of the departure from generally accepted accounting principles is not practicably determinable.

In our opinion, except for the effects of not capitalizing buildings and equipment or providing for depreciation on those assets as described in the preceding paragraph, the financial statements referred to above present fairly, in all material respects, the financial position of the Detroit Golf Club at August 31, 2000 and 1999 and the changes in its members' equity and its cash flows for the years then ended, in conformity with generally accepted accounting principles.

September 19, 2000   Plante & Moran, LLP

PROBLEMS

Problem 1

The Par More Course is a golf course open to the public. In addition to the short nine-hole course, it has a driving range and a miniature golf course. Its account balances for the month of May were as follows:

Green fees	$28,000
MGC sales	4,000
Driving range sales	1,500
Salaries expense	8,000
Wages expense	6,000
Supplies expense	3,000
Energy costs	1,500
Payroll taxes and benefits	2,000
Repairs expense	500
Depreciation expense	2,000
Interest expense	3,500
Income taxes (30% of pre-tax profit)	?

Required:
Prepare a simplified monthly income statement for the Par More Course.

Problem 2

R. Doe is the sole proprietor of Doe's Course. His balance sheet accounts are shown below as of the end of December 20X1.

Cash	$ 15,000
Prepaid insurance	1,000
Land	150,000
Accounts payable	8,000
Accounts receivable	10,000
Taxes payable	3,000
Mortgage payable—Long term	320,000
Equipment	200,000
Buildings	400,000
Mortgage payable—Current	40,000
Inventories	6,000
Wages payable	3,500
R. Doe, capital	??
Investments	50,000
Accumulated depreciation	200,000

Required:
Prepare the balance sheet for Doe's Course. Follow the example in Exhibit 2.3. *Note:* The amount of R. Doe, Capital is the difference between total assets and total liabilities.

MULTIPLE CHOICE QUESTIONS

1. Ideally, the golf course superintendent should receive _____ at the end of each accounting period, so that he/she is aware of the entire enterprise's operations and especially the role of the golf course.
   a. the balance sheet
   b. the income statement
   c. the operations budget
   d. a set of all the financial statements

2. The income statement shows the _____ of the enterprise.
   a. assets
   b. operating results
   c. liabilities
   d. owners' equity

3. Revenue (sales) should be recorded
   a. when cash is paid by the "customer" for services rendered.
   b. at the end of each month.
   c. when earned by the golf course.
   d. when the balance sheet is prepaid.

4. An enterprise's assets at the end of the month equal $1,000,000, while its owners' equity equals $600,000. Therefore, its _____ equals _____.
   a. revenues; $400,000
   b. expenses; $400,000
   c. liabilities; $1,600,000
   d. liabilities; $400,000

5. Inventories of supplies at the end of the accounting period are shown as _____ on the _____.
   a. an expense; balance sheet
   b. a liability; balance sheet
   c. a current asset; income statement
   d. a current asset; balance sheet

3

Basic Accounting Procedures and Records

This chapter focuses on the basic procedures used in the accounting process. In addition, accounting for inventories, depreciation, and payroll are briefly covered. A major purpose of this chapter is to provide an understanding of basic financial management. Chapter 2 presented the end product of the accounting process—the financial statements. Just how does the accounting system work that results in these statements?

THE ACCOUNTING PROCESS

In every business, transactions occur—that is, products and services are exchanged for cash. Employees who work for an enterprise provide services in exchange for a paycheck. When a business purchases water, it receives a good and pays cash. When a golfer plays a round of golf, the golf course provides a service and receives cash. The accounting process begins with basic transactions. Each transaction is analyzed and recorded in a journal. Since a journal is the first place the transaction is recorded (in a process sometimes called *journalizing*), the journal is referred to as the record of *original entry*. Transactions are generally recorded in the accounting department; however, the recording is based on transaction documents. The golf course superintendent is responsible for providing many of these documents, such as time cards for employees and receipts for purchases.

The accounting department maintains a journal for each type of transaction. For example, the payroll journal is used for recording employee checks, the check register is used for recording checks written to pay bills and invoices, and a purchases journal is used for recording purchases of goods or services on account. After transactions are recorded in journals, the amounts are transferred to ledger accounts.

A ledger is a collection of the accounts of the enterprise. One or more accounts are created for each line item on the Balance Sheet and the Income Statement. Accounts related to the Balance Sheet include Asset accounts, Liability accounts, and Owners' Equity accounts, while accounts related to the Income Statement include both Revenue and Expense accounts.

An enterprise might have a General Cash account and a Payroll Cash account; however, for reporting purposes these two accounts would generally be combined to reflect cash on the Balance Sheet at the end of the accounting period. Each account shows the net balance at a point in time based on the amounts transferred to the ledger accounts from the enterprise's journals. Each transaction influences the balance of various accounts. For example, when an employee is paid, the wages expense account increases and the cash account decreases.

The accounting department handles the processing of accounting information and maintaining of accounts. However, decisions made by the superintendent will affect the balances of various accounts.

At the end of the accounting period, accountants must prepare *adjusting entries* to reflect changes in accounts that have not previously been recorded. Examples include the accrual of payroll and the adjustment of inventories. A brief illustration of the payroll accrual is as follows:

A golf course pays its hourly employee on a biweekly basis. During the month of April employees are paid on April 14 and 28 for time worked for the two-week period through the 14th and 28th. However, employees also work the remaining days of April, that is, the 29th and 30th. Since these employees will not be paid for their work on April 29–30 until May 12, the accounting department accrues the wage expense for April 29–30 with an adjusting entry. Assume 100 hours are worked for the last two days of April and that the average hourly pay is $9.00. The payroll accrual would be to increase the appropriate wages expense accounts by $900 and to increase the wages payable account by $900.

Account balances as of the last day of the accounting period are reported on the financial statements. Often two or more similar accounts are combined, as previously stated.

The financial statements, as presented in Chapter 2, reflect the financial position (the Balance Sheet) and the results of operations (the Income Statement) for the golf course business. Several supporting schedules for profit, service, and cost centers supplement the financial statements. An in-depth discussion of the detailed schedule for the golf course maintenance department is provided in Chapter 4.

Special Reports and Analysis

Often, at the request of committees and/or the board of directors, special analytical reports are prepared. These reports provide detailed information for nonroutine decision making. For example, the decision to repair an old piece of equipment or buy a new one requires projections of repair costs of the old item and relevant costs of the new replacement. Alternatively, perhaps the amount of water usage is in question and the superintendent is requested to prepare a special report showing the usage on a monthly basis.

Consider how various records can be used to generate a report, using as an example the monthly water bill of a golf course. The superintendent's decisions about water usage will have a direct impact on the amount of the bill. The bill will be sent by the water company directly to the enterprise's accounting office, rather than to the superintendent. The accounting department will pay the bill, and record the payment in a journal. The payment will decrease the cash account and will increase the water expense account in the ledger. On a monthly basis, the balances in the various accounts in the ledger will be used to prepare the financial statements, including the Income Statement and the Balance Sheet. The water bill, as an expense, will reduce the profitability of the course, as shown on the Income Statement. The payment of the water bill reduces the amount of cash of the enterprise, as shown on the Balance Sheet. The superintendent or the course manager might want to analyze the rate of water usage. A special report can then be prepared, showing water usage per month and the resulting costs. Information for the reports would come from the financial records and possibly from the financial statements.

Exhibit 3.1 reflects the accounting process from actions resulting in transactions through the preparation of special reports.

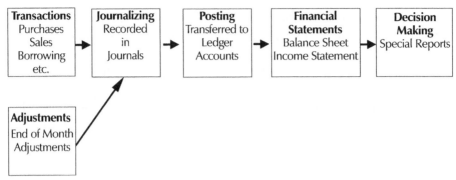

EXHIBIT 3.1. The Accounting Process

SPECIAL TOPICS TO AID IN UNDERSTANDING FINANCIAL STATEMENTS

To better understand accounting and the financial statements, let's look at two additional concepts: double entry accounting, and the cash and accrual methods of accounting.

Double Entry Accounting

The underlying idea of *double entry accounting* is that each business transaction will influence two or more accounts simultaneously. That is, a given transaction will (1) increase the balance of two or more accounts, (2) decrease the balance of two or more accounts, or (3) increase and decrease one or more accounts.

The double entry concept yields the specific process by which each transaction is entered into the financial records. It gives rise to the terms *debit* and *credit*. To debit or credit an account is to enter an amount into the account as a result of a transaction, thereby changing the balance of the account. The recording process is one in which one part of the transaction is entered on the left, or debit, side of an account, and the other part is entered on the right, or credit side of an account.

To use the previous example of the monthly water bill of a golf course (assume the water bill for the month totaled $1,000), consider the two accounts affected when the bill is paid. One account is the cash account from which the money is paid, and the other account is the water expense account, which reflects the use of the funds. The two accounts, and the two sides—left (debit) and right (credit)—can be illustrated:

Cash		Water Expense	
Debit	Credit	Debit	Credit
	$1,000	$1,000	

Two factors determine whether an amount should be debited or credited to the account. First, the nature of the transaction must be considered. That is, will there be an increase or a decrease in the account balance? In the water bill example above, cash is decreased and expenses are increased. Second, the type of account impacted will also determine whether to debit or credit. Recall that there are five basic types of accounts:

1. **Revenues** from the sale of goods or services, shown on the Income Statement
2. **Expenses**, or costs, shown on the Income Statement
3. **Assets**, what the course owns, shown on the Balance Sheet
4. **Liabilities**, what the course owes others, shown on the Balance Sheet
5. **Equity**, the net worth of owners, shown on the Balance Sheet

Keeping track of these two factors requires some memory, and perhaps a change in thinking from what may be customary. The rules are as follows:

	Debit	**Credit**
Asset accounts	Increases	Decreases
Expense accounts	Increases	Decreases
Revenue accounts	Decreases	Increases
Liability accounts	Decreases	Increases
Equity accounts	Decreases	Increases

The normal balance of an account is what increases the account. For example, the cash account is increased with a debit entry; therefore, the cash account normally has a debit balance. If the cash account has a credit balance, the records reveal that the cash account is negative; that is, cash has been *overdrawn*. Needless to say, this is cause for alarm and some quick action! The normal balance of each type of account is as follows:

Asset accounts	Debit
Liability accounts	Credit
Owners' Equity accounts	Credit
Revenue accounts	Credit
Expense accounts	Debit

For each transaction, one or more accounts will be debited while one or more accounts will be credited. Also, the sum of the amounts of the debit entries must equal the total of accounts credited.

The normal balance of the Asset, Liability, and Owners' Equity accounts reflects the balance of the accounting equation and the fact that debits must equal credits, as follows:

$$\text{Assets} = \text{Liabilities} + \text{Owners' Equity}$$

$$\text{(Debits)} = \text{(Credits)} + \quad \text{(Credits)}$$

The basic accounting equation reflects only Balance Sheet accounts. The net income for the accounting period, as shown on the enterprise's Income Statement, is closed into the appropriate Owners' Equity account. When the enterprise achieves a profit, the impact on owners' equity is an increase. Therefore, the accounting equation can be expanded as follows:

$$\text{Assets} = \text{Liabilities} + \text{Owners' Equity}$$

$$\overbrace{+\text{Revenues} - \text{Expenses}}$$

or

$$\text{Assets} = \text{Liabilities} + \text{Owners' Equity} + \text{Revenues} - \text{Expenses}$$

The objective of this double entry process is to make a record of all aspects of the transaction, such that the accounting equation remains in balance. Affected accounts may be on the Balance Sheet and/or the Income Statement. For example, consider the following three transactions:

1. Purchase of $500 in supplies to be placed in inventory with cash of $100 down and the remaining $400 on credit. The journal entry would be:

	Debit	Credit
Inventory (increase asset)	$500	
Cash (decrease asset)		$100
Accounts Payable (increase liability)		400

Notice that the sum of debits ($500) equals the sum of credits ($500). Two asset accounts and one liability account were affected by this transaction. Also notice how the accounting equation remains in balance as a result of the transaction, as is true for all entries.

$$\underline{Assets} = \underline{Liabilities} + \underline{Owners'Equity}$$
$$Inventory - Cash = Liabilities$$
$$\$500 - \$100 = \$400$$

2. Payment of $2,000 in wages. The journal entry is:

Wages expense (increase expense) $2,000
Cash (decrease asset) $2,000

The accounting equation remains in balance:

$$\underline{Asset} = \underline{Liabilities} + \underline{Owners'\ Equity} + \underline{Revenue} - \underline{Expenses}$$

Cash =   Wages Expense
–$2,000 =   –$2,000

The impact of this transaction will be reflected on both of the primary financial statements. Salary expense will be shown on the Income Statement and will reduce net income. The cash reduction will be shown on the Balance Sheet, as a reduction in total assets. This may be true for many of the decisions made by the superintendent. That is, a single decision may impact both profitability of the course as well as the financial position of the enterprise, as shown on the Balance Sheet.

3. Green fees of $200 are received from party of golfers. The journal entry would be:

Cash (increase asset) $200
Green Fees (increase revenue) $200

Again, the accounting equation is in balance:

$$\underline{Cash} = \underline{Liabilities} + \underline{Equity} + \underline{Revenues} - \underline{Expenses}$$
$$+\$200 = \qquad\qquad +\$200$$

The double entry process records all impacts of a transaction because the balance in each account affected by the transaction is adjusted. The account balance is determined by adding all items that increase the balance and then subtracting from the sum all items that decrease the balance. Thus, the balance summarizes in numerical form all the transactions that affect that account.

Cash and Accrual Methods of Accounting

There are two distinctly different methods of accounting. The simplest method—used only by the smallest of businesses (generally not golf course enterprises)—is the cash method. Under the cash method, revenue is recognized when cash is received for sales, fees, and so on, and expenses are recognized when cash is expended for goods purchased and services used in operations.

For example, the sale of a good would be recognized, using the cash method, only when the cash is received. So if a customer purchased a good in one month but paid for it in the following month, the sale is recognized in the following month. In addition, expenses are recognized when cash is disbursed under the cash method. If a piece of equipment is purchased, the cost is expensed when it is paid for. Even though the piece of equipment may benefit the business for several years, expense is recognized when cash is disbursed.

In contrast, the accrual method of accounting recognizes revenues when earned and recognizes expense when incurred. This results in many transactions being recorded, even though no current exchange of cash takes place.

Consider the difference in cash and accrual accounting for two transactions. A club member charges a party costing $800 to his account on April 1. The club member pays his account of $800 on May 15.

Transactions	Cash Method	Accrual Method	
April 1			
Club member charges $800 party to his account.	No entry (no cash was exchanged)	Accounts Rec. Sales	$800 $800
May 15			
Club member pays off his account.	Cash $800 Sales $800	Cash Accounts Rec.	$800 $800

Under the cash method, the Income Statement for April would not reflect the sales activity. However, in May the sales activity is shown on an Income Statement based on the cash method.

Under the accrual method, sales are recognized when they occur, and a corresponding receivable is recorded. In the following month the receivable is reduced by the cash paid.

In the above example, the difference between the two methods is eliminated over a two-month period. However, consider the difference in accounting for equipment. Under the cash method, equipment purchased is expensed when it is paid for, while under the accrual method the cost of equipment is expensed over the expected life of the equipment. If the equipment has a five-year life, then the differences between the Income Statements following these two approaches for this item alone would be reflected over five years.

Under the accrual method, expenses are matched with the revenue they help generate, regardless of when cash is disbursed. For example, a $20,000 expenditure for a utility truck is initially recorded as an asset and depreciated (expensed) over its useful life. Because the truck will be used for several years to generate sales, it follows that the cost of the truck should be matched against the sales as an expense over several years. A more detailed discussion of depreciation accounting will be provided later in this chapter.

There is no specific business transaction to trigger the recording of depreciation or the adjustments of several other accounts required by the accrual method of accounting. Therefore, at the end of each month, the accounting staff prepares adjusting entries (mentioned previously in this chapter) to recognize the expense. For example, a fire insurance premium of $12,000 was paid on January 1, 20X1, for the year of 20X1. The $12,000 was recorded in the prepaid insurance account (an asset). At the end of each month, 1/12, or $1,000, of prepaid insurance is recognized as an expense by an adjusting entry to decrease the prepaid insurance amount and to increase insurance expense.

Benefits of the Accrual Method of Accounting

This discussion suggests that the accrual method of accounting is more desirable if the accounting system is to provide the information useful for planning and control within the enterprise. The following conditions require the accrual method of accounting to be used in order to be able to match expenses with revenue:

1. **Seasonal fluctuations.** When expenditures are made far in advance of the revenue they generate, it is necessary to allocate the cost of the expenditures to the periods in which the related revenues are generated. Similarly, cash received in advance of the delivery of goods or services must be spread over the periods of delivery. Both of these conditions are prevalent at a golf course. In turn, this creates a need to have a separation of the revenue and the cash accounts in order to allow proper accounting for timing differences.

2. **High inventory.** When the purchase of inventory is a substantial expenditure of the course, it is necessary to recognize the cost of the inventory bought in one period as it is sold or used in subsequent

periods. This creates a need for a way to account for differences in timing between the acquisition and the use of inventory items. Accounting for inventory will be discussed in more detail later in this chapter.

3. **High equipment levels.** When the course owns a large amount of equipment, it is necessary to match equipment cost with the sales that are generated over the life of the equipment. This is achieved by means of depreciation expense.

4. **Extension of credit.** When credit is extended to golfers, it is necessary to recognize the sale in the period when it was made, not when payment is required. This difference in timing may be significant, as illustrated previously. Under accrual accounting, revenue and the receivable are recorded at the time of sale.

The accrual basis of accounting offers many benefits to the owner–manager of a club. Its primary benefit is the information provided by the matching concept. In addition, accrual-based financial statements are more comparable from period to period than are those prepared under the cash basis.

ACCOUNTING FOR INVENTORY

Inventory consists of various items held for resale and/or to be used within the enterprise. In a club's food service operation, inventories include food and beverage for resale and paper supplies, such as napkins. The pro shop of the golf course would have an extensive inventory of goods for sale. The superintendent would be responsible for inventories of supplies to operate and maintain the golf course, including fertilizer, chemicals, and fuel.

Inventory on hand at the end of the accounting period is shown on the enterprise's Balance Sheet. It is generally reported at cost, except when the market value is lower than cost. Since inventory is expected to be sold or used within 12 months from the Balance Sheet date, it is shown as a current asset on the enterprise's Balance Sheet.

The major objective of inventory management is control. Inventory control is accomplished by having the right amount of inventory available to meet the demand of buyers and/or to use in the business. For example, on one hand, too little fertilizer on hand results in *stockouts*, that is, an insufficient amount available for the work to be accomplished. On the other hand, too much fertilizer results in excessive amounts to be carried over to the following year. The superintendent must carefully project the inventory needs of the course and order the optimal amounts on a timely basis.

It might not be economical to order all the desired inventory for the year at one time, because the costs to carry the inventory might exceed the benefit of having it available throughout the entire season. As long as suppliers can provide the inventory items on a timely basis, inventory is often stocked only for its use over a short period of time. However, the superintendent must also consider volume discounts as part of purchasing plans. Sizable discounts are often available to enterprises that purchase large quantities of supplies, especially when they purchase them at the beginning of the season. The amount of cost savings from these discounts related to major up-front purchases might more than offset the increased costs of carrying the large inventories.

Periodically, a physical count of inventoried items is taken, and after a comparison against the estimated usage is made, orders are placed for the additional items required. Also, at the end of the enterprise's year a physical inventory is taken to determine the amount of inventory on hand, which will be reported on the enterprise's Balance Sheet.

The larger the golf course operation, the greater the need to use more sophisticated inventory control systems. Increasingly, golf course inventory control systems are computerized. Inventory is recorded on the computer when purchased and then reduced by the computer as sales occur. The computer reveals the amount of inventory that should be on hand at the end of the accounting period. Still, a physical inventory must be taken at the end of the accounting period to verify the inventory numbers provided by the computer. Any differences are accounted for by the accounting department.

As inventory is sold or used in the business, inventory is expensed; that is, the cost of the inventory is moved from the Balance Sheet (as an asset) to the Income Statement (as an expense). The expensing of inventory held for resale is called *cost of goods sold*, while the expense of supplies, such as fertilizer, used by a course is simply called fertilizer expense.

The equation for determining the cost of goods sold is as follows:

+ cost of inventory at beginning of period
+ purchases of inventory
= goods available for sale
− ending inventory (physical count)
= cost of goods sold

For example, consider a course's snack bar, which started the month of June with a beginning inventory of $1,000 of food for resale. During June, several purchases of food totaled $3,000. The physical inventory at the end of June totaled $800. The cost of goods sold is determined as follows:

Beginning inventory (6/1)	$1,000
Purchases during June	3,000
Foods available	4,000
Ending inventory (6/30)	800
Cost of food sold	$3,200

Since items purchased for the inventory during an accounting period may have different costs, even for the same item, the question revolves around placing a value on the items remaining in the inventory at the end of the accounting period. Since this impacts the value placed on the goods taken from inventory, it impacts the expense for the period.

One method presumes that the item used from inventory is from the last purchase of inventory made. Another method presumes that the item used was from the first order made. Still another method is based on identifying the specific cost with the inventory item sold or used. During periods of stable prices, these three assumptions yield the same value for the inventory used. However, in times of increasing or decreasing prices for inventory, the three assumptions yield different values for the items used. Thus, the inventory costing assumption chosen will affect the value placed on inventory used (cost of goods sold or supplies expense) shown on the Income Statement, as well as the balance in the inventory account shown on the Balance Sheet.

1. The **FIFO (first-in, first-out)** assumption assigns a cost to goods sold or used equal to the cost of the earliest items bought that are still on hand. If the price of inventory items is increasing, this will result in using a lower value for supplies expense and will effectively result in a higher net income than if other methods are used. It will also mean that the value assigned to the goods remaining in inventory will be higher and nearer to their current price, yielding a higher inventory balance on the Balance Sheet.

2. The **LIFO (last-in, first-out)** assumption assigns a cost to goods sold or used equal to the cost of the last items bought in the current period. In a period during which price of inventory items is rising, the value of ending inventory on the Balance Sheet will be understated, since it is based on costs that existed earlier when costs were lower than current costs. Also, costs or expenses will be greater in a period of rising prices compared to FIFO, thus effectively resulting in a lower net income.

3. The **specific identification method** assigns a cost to goods sold or used equal to the cost of the item used. With this approach, the cost related to the item must be marked on the item when received so the exact cost can be identified when the items are sold or used.

These cost approaches are illustrated in Exhibit 3.2. Notice the differences in the cost of Power Bars sold. FIFO resulted in the lowest cost of goods sold and the highest cost of inventory at the end of the month, while LIFO resulted in the highest cost of Power Bars sold and the lowest inventory cost at the end of the month. This simplified example reveals relatively minor differences; however, when considered for hundreds of items of inventory, differences become more significant.

An attempt should be made to select the inventory costing assumption that most closely patterns the actual flow of inventory goods. If inventory consists of pesticides, the FIFO assumption would probably be used, because the oldest (first-in) would likely be used before the more recent shipment. Conversely, an inventory of sand stored in a huge pile would probably be valued using the LIFO method. Since sand would be removed from the top of the pile first (first-out), the most recent purchase (last-in) would be used first.

The hypothetical Green Golf Club sells a popular Power Bar at its snack bar. The inventory and cost of the Power Bars on June 1 were 10 bars costing $0.15 each ($1.50 in total). Purchases of the Power Bar during June were as follows:

Date	Number of Bars Purchased	Cost per Bar	Total
June 7	50	$0.16	$ 8.00
June 12	100	0.17	17.00
June 27	50	0.18	9.00
Total	200		$34.00

A physical count on June 30 indicated 10 bars in inventory. Cost of Power Bars Sold: Specific

Identification	FIFO	LIFO	Specific Identification
Beginning Inventory	$ 1.50	$ 1.50	$ 1.50
Purchases	34.00	34.00	34.00
Available	35.50	35.50	35.50
Ending Inventory	1.80 (1)	1.50 (2)	1.75 (3)
Cost of Power Bars Sold	$33.70	$34.00	$33.75

(1) 10 bars @ $0.18 = $1.80
(2) 10 bars @ $0.15 = $1.50
(3) Ending inventory revealed 5 bars costing $0.18 each and 5 bars costing $0.17 each.

EXHIBIT 3.2. Different Inventory Cost Approaches

At some golf enterprises, some types of inventories of supplies are insignificant. When this is the case, the supplies are expensed when purchased and no inventory of supplies is reported on the enterprise's Balance Sheet at the end of the accounting period.

ACCOUNTING FOR PROPERTY AND EQUIPMENT

Property and equipment includes the land, land improvements, buildings, furniture, and equipment owned by the golf course enterprise. The nature of these assets, often called fixed assets, are that (1) these items are expected to have useful lives in excess of one year, (2) they are tangible, and (3) they are used in the business to generate revenues.

The useful life is determined by management. The superintendent is generally in the best position to indicate the expected useful lives of the various pieces of golf course maintenance equipment.

Property and equipment usually represent the largest dollar value of the asset section of the golf enterprise's Balance Sheet. As these items are used in the business, their cost is expensed through the process of depreciation.

Acquisitions of property and equipment are generally approved by the governing board of the enterprise, based on a carefully prepared capital budgeting plan. Capital budgeting will be discussed in more detail in Chapter 8. The determination between capitalizing an expenditure— that is, recording it as property and equipment or expensing it—should be established by the governing board. For example, the board may set a cutoff of $200 for office furniture and equipment. Thus, a lawnmower that costs $420 is recorded as equipment and will be depreciated over the next several years. A hand shovel costing $40 will be immediately expensed, even though the operation may use this item as long as it will the mower. The difference is the relative cost of each. For control purposes, some operations attach an inventory number to each piece of equipment and furniture. A file is maintained for each item, with the item's identification number, description, serial number if available, date acquired, purchase cost, and details regarding depreciation of the item.

The superintendent must also determine whether a major repair of a piece of equipment is recorded as an expense or as an increase in the equipment account. Such expenditures theoretically should be recorded as an increase in the equipment account (and subsequently depreciated) when the life of the equipment is increased.

The cost of the battery replaced in a tractor would generally be expensed, while the cost of the overhaul of the tractor's engine would often be capitalized—that is, recorded as an increase in the appropriate equipment account. Superintendents need to establish guidelines and be consistent in their application in regard to their decisions to expense or capitalize these types of expenditures.

At least annually, a physical inventory of the property and equipment under the superintendent's control should be taken. Any difference between the physical inventory and the inventory according to the accounting records should be investigated and accounted for.

The expensing of property and equipment is referred to as *depreciation*. The accountant records depreciation for the business by debiting *Depreciation Expense* and crediting *Accumulated Depreciation*. The amount of depreciation expense for the accounting period is shown on the Income Statement and the accumulated depreciation is offset against the property and equipment on the Balance Sheet to reflect the net book value of property and equipment at the end of the accounting period.

The amount of depreciation expense of an item for the accounting period is based on (1) the cost of the item to be depreciated, (2) the estimated useful life of the item, (3) the salvage value of the item, and (4) the method of depreciation used.

The cost is the amount the item was recorded at when it was purchased. The useful life of the item is the estimated period of time the item is expected to be used. The salvage value is the expected disposal value at the end of the useful life of the item. The method of depreciation used is one of several acceptable methods. The most commonly used depreciation methods are the straight-line method, double-declining-balance method, and sum-of-the-years'-digits method. The Internal Revenue Service allows the use of the method called the Modified Accelerated Cost Recovery System (MACRS) for computing depreciation expense. Although the MACRS method is used for income tax reporting, one of the other methods is often used for financial reporting. However, using different methods for taxes and reporting purposes requires keeping two sets of depreciation records for each depreciable asset.

The three methods of depreciation to be presented will be briefly described and illustrated:

1. **Straight-line method**. An equal amount of depreciation expense is calculated for each year as follows:

$$\text{Depreciation expense} = \frac{\text{cost} - \text{salvage value}}{\text{years of useful life}}$$

2. **Double-declining-balance method**. The rate of depreciation is double that of the straight-line rate and is applied to the undepreciated cost of the asset as follows:

$$\text{Depreciation expense} = \frac{2}{n} \times \text{undepreciated cost}$$

(n = estimated life in years)

3. **Sum-of-the-years'-digits method**. This method also results in greater depreciation in the earlier years of the asset's life. The annual depreciation is determined as follows:

$$\text{Depreciation expense} = (\text{cost} - \text{salvage value})\left(\frac{RL}{n(n+1)/2}\right)$$

where RL = remaining life in years at the beginning of the year and n = estimated life in years

Exhibit 3.3 contains an illustration of the calculation of depreciation using the three methods discussed above. Notice that each method results in $18,000 of depreciation expense over the five-year period. However, double-declining-balance results in the greatest amount of depreciation in the first year of the three methods and the least amount in 2005. This illustration clearly shows why the double-declining-balance and sum-of-the-years'-digits methods are called *accelerated methods* because the amounts of depreciation are greater for the earlier years than is the case when the depreciation expense is calculated per the straight-line method.

As with inventory costing assumptions, discussed earlier, the choice of depreciation methods should be carefully made. The depreciation method used should reflect the characteristics of the property and equipment being depreciated and attempt to match depreciation expense with revenues generated by the use of the asset. For instance, office furniture likely will generate revenues evenly over the periods it is used. In order to best match the cost of the furniture with revenues, it is probably logical to use the straight-line method, which produces equal amounts of depreciation expense each period. Some equipment, however, performs better in the early years of its life and becomes less productive in later years. One of the accelerated methods might be used in this instance to attempt a match of expenses with revenues. If it is difficult to determine which method is most appropriate, simplicity should take precedence, and the straight-line method would be an appropriate choice.

Assume the Blue Golf Course purchases a truck for $20,000 on January 1, 2001. The truck has an estimated useful life of five years and an estimated salvage value of $2,000. The annual depreciation for 2001–2005 for each of the three methods is as follows:

	Straight-line	Double-declining-balance	Sum-of-the-years'-digits
2001	$ 3,600 (1)	$ 8,000 (2)	$ 6,000 (3)
2002	3,600	4,800	4,800
2003	3,600	2,880	3,600
2004	3,600	1,728	2,400
2005	3,600	592	1,200
Total	$18,000	$18,000	$18,000

(1) $$\frac{C-SV}{n}; \quad \frac{20,000-2,000}{5} = \$3,600$$

(2) $$\text{undepreciated cost}\left(\frac{2}{n}\right);$$
$$2001 = 20,000 \times 2/5 = \$8,000$$
$$2002 = 12,000 \times 0.4 = \$4,800$$
$$2003 = 7,200 \times 0.4 = \$2,880$$
$$2004 = 4,320 \times 0.4 = \$1,728$$
$$2005 = 2,592 - 2,000 = \$ 592$$

(3) $$(C-SV)\left(\frac{RL}{n(n+1)/2}\right);$$
$$2001: \quad (20,000-2,000)(5/15) = \$6,000$$
$$2002: \quad 18,000(4/15) = \$4,800$$
$$2003: \quad 18,000(3/15) = \$3,600$$
$$2004: \quad 18,000(2/15) = \$2,400$$
$$2005: \quad 18,000(1/15) = \$1,200$$

EXHIBIT 3.3. Illustration of Calculation of Depreciation

ACCOUNTING FOR PAYROLL

Payroll expenses are the largest expenditure of funds at most golf course enterprises. A recent annual statistical report from PKF International revealed that 69 percent of the total golf course maintenance expenses went to payroll. For the average country club, the payroll expenses approximated 46 percent of total revenues. By comparison the average total revenues and total payroll expenses for a daily fee course in the United States in 2000 were $922,000 and $325,000, respectively, according to the National Golf Foundation. Thus, payroll costs for daily fee courses were 32.8 percent of total revenues.

Just what is included in payroll costs? Salaries, wages, employee benefits, and all payroll taxes are recorded as payroll expenses. Often an enterprise will report on their Income Statement salaries and wages separate from employee benefits and payroll taxes. The superintendent may desire to have several accounts established to allow him/her to track the payroll expenses.

There are entire books written about human resources—that is, the hiring, training, supervising, and terminating of employees. Personnel is the most critical element in a service business such as a golf course. Although machinery and supplies are important in maintaining the golf course, these must be properly managed by people.

The focus on this section will be minimum wages, calculating payroll, recording payroll, and accruing payroll.

The Fair Labor Standards Act (FLSA)—commonly known as the Federal Wage and Labor Law—covers, among other things, minimum wage and overtime pay. Most golf course operations will be subject to this law. However, if the state where the course is located has a more stringent law than the FLSA, such as higher minimum wages, generally the enterprise will have to comply with the state law.

The federal minimum wage is currently $5.15 per hour; that is, the enterprise must pay their employees a minimum of $5.15, and 1.5 times the employees' hourly rate for each overtime hour. Assume a hypothetical Green Golf Club has an employee (Bob Smith) earning $240 during the regular work week, which is a 40-hour period. The regular hourly rate for this employee is determined to be $6.00 ($240/40 = $6.00). Therefore, if Bob worked 48 hours during the work week, his gross pay would be determined as follows:

$$\text{Overtime rate} = \text{regular hourly rate} \times 1.5$$
$$= \$6.00 \times 1.5$$
$$= \underline{\underline{\$9.00}}$$

$$\text{Gross pay} = (\text{regular hours} \times \text{regular hourly rate})$$
$$+ (\text{overtime hours} \times \text{overtime rate})$$
$$= (40 \times \$6.00) + (8 \times \$9.00)$$
$$= 240 + 72 = \underline{\$312}$$

Needless to say, overtime pay drives the average pay upward. In the prior example, Bob's regular hourly pay was $6.00 per hour; however, his average pay rate for 48 hours of work was $6.40 per hour ($312/48 = $6.40) and this average hourly rate would continue to increase as overtime hours increase.

In addition to gross pay, enterprises must pay social security taxes and Medicare taxes as required by the Federal Insurance Contributions Act, simply referred to as FICA. The current FICA tax is 7.65 percent on the first $87,000 of wages and 1.45 percent on wages in excess of $87,000. On Bob's wages the FICA tax on his gross wages is $23.87, determined as follows:

$$\text{FICA tax} = \text{gross wages} \times \text{FICA tax rate}$$
$$= \$312 \times 7.65\%$$
$$= \underline{\$23.87}$$

The FICA tax must be withheld from the employee's gross pay and an equal amount must be paid by the golf course operation. Income taxes must also be withheld from the employee's gross pay. Some courses are located in cities and states that require income taxes to be withheld as well.

Some enterprises allow their employees to purchase health and other benefits by having amounts deducted from their paychecks. Thus, the difference between an employee's gross wages and the net wage may be substantial.

The payroll for the pay period is determined based on salaries and hourly wages times the hours worked. Generally, an enterprise uses a time clock for recording time worked by employees paid an hourly wage. The time cards should be approved for the pay period by the superintendent and forwarded to the accounting department for processing. The payroll clerk determines the gross pay, income tax and FICA withholdings, deductions for benefits, and net pay. Each paycheck is recorded in the payroll journal by accounting department personnel and charged to the appropriate department. The recording of Bob Smith's check, assuming 20 percent of the gross pay is withheld for federal income tax purposes, would be as follows:

Wages—golf course maintenance $312.00
    FICA payable $ 23.87
    Federal income taxes payable   62.40
    Payroll cash   225.73

It is important to understand the difference between gross pay and net pay. Smith's gross pay, in this example, is $312.00, while the amount of his paycheck is only $225.73. The difference is taxes of $86.27, which have been withheld and will be paid to the appropriate tax authorities. When other items such as the employee's cost of health care premiums are subtracted, the difference between gross and net becomes even greater.

In addition, the payroll clerk would also record the FICA tax expense as follows:

Payroll taxes—golf course maintenance $ 23.87
    FICA payable $ 23.87

Thus, the total payroll expense related to Bob's pay and the FICA tax is $335.87. The course pays Bob $225.73 and owes the federal government the remaining $110.14 (federal income taxes of $62.40 plus FICA taxes of $47.74).

Finally, any unpaid salaries and wages at the end of the accounting period must be recorded in order to match expenses with revenues, based on the accrual method of accounting. This recording is accomplished by using an adjusting entry, as discussed earlier in this chapter. The accounting department estimates the unpaid gross wages and records the payroll expense and the related liability. Assume that for the last three days of the accounting period Bob Smith worked 24 hours for which he has not been paid. Then the payroll accrual related to Bob's hours worked would be calculated and recorded as follows:

Wages—golf course maintenance $144.00
    Payroll taxes—golf course maintenance   11.02
    Accrued wages and taxes $155.02

Note: The wages are determined by multiplying the hourly rate of $6.00 by 24 hours and the FICA tax recorded in the payroll is determined by multiplying the gross wages of $144.00 by 7.65 percent.

The accounting department processes the payroll, but the superintendent's role in managing employees of his/her cost center is critical to controlling payroll expenses, which directly affect the golf course maintenance department.

SUMMARY

The accounting process begins with the analysis of business transactions to determine how they will be recorded, and results in financial statements, including the Balance Sheet and the Income Statement. Management will use information in the financial statements in making decisions to effectively manage their golf course.

The accounting process entails double entry accounting, which means every transaction impacts two or more accounts. The double entry system includes the concepts of debit and credit. Two different approaches to accounting are *cash* and *accrual*. The accrual approach is preferred, as it recognizes revenue when earned and expense when incurred. The cash approach results in recognition of revenue expense when cash flows occur.

Finally, in this chapter, accounting for inventory, property and equipment, and payroll was covered. The superintendent is directly involved in managing these three major resources to provide services to users of the golf course.

PROBLEMS

Problem 1

The Red Golf Club purchases a fairway mower for the golf course superintendent's use on January 1, 20X2. The cost is $35,000; the mower is expected to have a useful life of five years and a salvage value of $5,000.

Required:
1. Determine the depreciation expense for 20X2 using the straight-line method.
2. Determine the depreciation expense for 20X2 using the sum-of-the-years'-digits method.
3. What is the difference between the total depreciation for the five years of 20X2–20X6 when the straight-line and sum-of-the-years'-digits methods are used?

Problem 2

Susan Woods is a full-time employee of Red Golf Course. For a 40-hour week her gross pay was $300.00. During the week ended June 7, she worked 50 hours. Assume the following:
1. The FICA tax rate is 7.65 percent on gross wages.
2. Income taxes withheld from her gross pay are as follows:
   a. federal withholding: 20%
   b. state withholding: 5%

Further, assume that at the end of June she worked 24 hours, for which she will be paid in July.

Required:
1. Determine Susan's regular pay rate.
2. Determine Susan's overtime pay rate.
3. Determine Susan's gross and net wages for the week of June 7.
4. Prepare the adjusting entry to accrue unpaid wages and related taxes at the end of June.

MULTIPLE CHOICE QUESTIONS

1. A ledger is
   a. like a journal, as checks are initially recorded in it.
   b. a collection of accounts of the enterprise.
   c. a book for maintaining employee time-records.
   d. an obsolete accounting tool.

2. Double entry accounting
   a. increases the balance of two or more accounts.
   b. decreases the balance of two or more accounts.
   c. increases and decreases the balance of one or more accounts.
   d. all of the above.

3. Which type of account listed below normally has a debit balance?
   a. liability account
   b. revenue account
   c. asset account
   d. owners' equity account

4. The basic accounting equation is
   a. assets – owners' equity = liabilities
   b. assets + liabilities = owners' equity
   c. assets = liabilities + owners' equity
   d. assets + owners' equity = liabilities

5. A mowing machine costing $10,000 will have a useful life of five years. The estimated salvage value is $1,000. Assets are depreciated using the straight-line method. What is the depreciation expense for the first year of the equipment's life?
   a. $10,000
   b. $5,000
   c. $2,000
   d. $1,800

4

Golf Course Operations Schedule

The Income Statement for many golf course enterprises includes several supporting schedules, as shown in Exhibit 2.4. These supporting schedules are for the profit, service, and cost centers of the business. They provide detailed information to allow the managers of each center to quickly determine how well they have managed their departments from a financial perspective. The focus of this chapter is the golf course operations schedule. This portion of the enterprise's Income Statement is the responsibility of the superintendent. Superintendents should have intimate knowledge of this schedule, as it reveals from a financial perspective their performance. Further, when the actual results for the period are compared to the budget, the operations schedule becomes the basis for further analysis and possibly future action.

Exhibit 4.1 is the schedule for golf course maintenance from the uniform systems of accounts published by the Club Managers Association of America (CMAA). Labeled "Schedule 9," it is one of 19 potential schedules that support a club's Income Statement. Other schedules provided for in the uniform system of accounts for clubs include golf shop, food, beverages, clubhouse, and energy costs, just to list a few. This schedule will be discussed in detail; however, for comparative purposes Exhibit 4.2 is the recommended schedule for golf course operations from the uniform system of accounts for clubs published by the National Golf Course Owners Association (NGCOA). The major differences are as follows:

Departmental Expenses

    Payroll and related expenses

        Salaries and wages $ _____

        Payroll taxes and employee benefits

        Employees' meals   _____

            Total payroll and related expenses   _____

    Other expenses

        Applicants

        Computer expense

        Dues and subscriptions

        Energy costs

        Equipment rental

        Fertilizer

        Gasoline and lubricants

        Laundry and linen

        Licenses and permits

        Operating supplies

        Printing and stationery

        Professional development

        Refuse removal

        Repairs and maintenance

            Course buildings

            Drainage systems

            Fences and bridges

            Irrigation systems

            Mowers, tractors, and trucks

            Roads and paths

        Sand and top dressing

        Seeds, flowers, and shrubs

        Small tools

        Telephone

        Topsoil

        Tree care

        Uniforms

        Vehicle expense

        Water

        Other operating expenses   _____

            Total other expenses   _____

TOTAL GOLF COURSE MAINTENANCE EXPENSES $ _____

EXHIBIT 4.1. Blank Country Club Golf Course Maintenance, Schedule 9

Income

   Daily greens fees $

   Annual green fees/members fees   _____

      Total income   _____

Departmental Expenses

  Payroll and related expenses

   Salaries and wages

    Course maintenance

    Golf professionals and staff

   Payroll taxes and employee benefits   _____

     Total payroll and related expenses   _____

Other Expenses

  Grounds and greens supplies

   Fertilizer, insecticides, and topsoil

   Gasoline and lubricants

   Sand and gravel

   Seeds, flowers, plants, and shrubs

   Other supplies

  Pro, starter, and caddy supplies and expenses

  Repairs

    Course buildings

    Fences and bridges

    Mowers, tractors, and trucks

    Roads and paths

    Water and drainage systems

  Uniforms

  Energy costs

  Miscellaneous   _____

   Total other expenses   _____

   Total departmental expenses   _____

   Department income (loss)   _____

Note: Complimentary rounds are recorded as income with daily greens fees in the golf course operations and as an expense in the advertising and sales promotion schedule.

EXHIBIT 4.2. Golf Course Operations, Schedule I

NGCOA's format includes two revenue lines, whereas CMAA's schedule for golf course maintenance includes only expenses. NGCOA's schedule includes salaries and wages for the golf professionals and staff, as well as related supplies and expenses. These salaries and wages and related expenses are shown on the golf shop schedule under CMAA's uniform system. The other expenses shown on these schedules are somewhat the same, though the CMAA schedule has more classifications.

Regardless of the accounting system used, the Income Statement and the related schedules should be sufficiently detailed to enhance management's performance.

EXPENSES

The golf course maintenance schedule (Exhibit 4.1) is divided between payroll and related expenses, and other expenses. The other expenses include all other direct expenses of maintaining the golf course.

Payroll and Related Expenses

Payroll and related expenses include salaries and wages and the related expenses of employee benefits and payroll taxes and employee meals. All expenses reported in this section are incurred during the accounting period, whether or not they have been paid.

Salaries and wages include the gross pay of all golf course maintenance personnel, including the superintendent and his or her work force. Superintendents who desire additional classifications in these or other areas should discuss the need for additional information with the controller to have this schedule adapted for their use.

Payroll taxes consist primarily of FICA taxes, while employee benefits include vacation time, sick leave, workers' compensation, unemployment costs, health insurance, life insurance, pension, and the superintendent's expense allowance. Any contributions by personnel toward the cost of fringe benefits are offset against the gross payments so that only the cost to the golf course enterprise is shown.

The third line under payroll and related expenses is Employee Meals. The cost of employee meals provided to course maintenance personnel by the golf course is recorded in this account.

The total payroll and related expenses of golf courses is often the largest expense of the operation. It is imperative that superintendents effectively manage personnel to optimize services of the work force while adequately controlling this area of expenses.

Other Expenses

All other direct expenses of the golf course operation are shown in this section of the schedule. A brief line-by-line discussion goes as follows:

Applicants. The cost of insecticides, pesticides, and similar chemicals used to maintain the golf course should be charged to this account.

Computer Expense. This item includes all expenses related to computer usage, including repairs and service contracts, supplies, and minor replacements. Major replacements should be capitalized and depreciated.

Dues and Subscriptions. This account should be charged with the cost of memberships, subscriptions to newspaper magazines and books used by employees in golf course maintenance department.

Equipment Rental. The cost of equipment rented for use in the golf course maintenance department should be charged to this account.

Energy Costs. The cost of electricity and other energy used by the golf course maintenance department should be charged to this account.

Fertilizer. The cost of fertilizer should be charged to this account.

Gasoline and Lubricants. The cost of gasoline and lubricants for equipment and by the golf course maintenance department is charged to this account.

Laundry and Linen. This account should included the laundry costs assigned to the department.

Licenses and Permits. Licenses and Permits includes the cost of licenses and permits required by the golf course maintenance department.

Operating Supplies. Operating Supplies includes the cost of cleaning supplies, and similar operating expenses applicable to the golf course maintenance department. If the cost of any of these items is significant, items and amounts should be listed separately from Operating Supplies.

Printing and Stationery. This cost of printed forms, service manuals, stationery, and office supplies that are purchased from outside printers or produced internally should be charged to this account when they are used by employees of the golf course maintenance department.

Professional Development. Professional development includes costs other than time associated with training beverage employees. Examples include the costs of training materials, supplies, instructor fees and outside seminars and conferences.

Refuse Removal. This account is used for recording the cost of waste removal.

Repairs and Maintenance. Several accounts will generally be used to record the repairs and maintenance of specific assets. The recommended accounts are course buildings; drainage systems; fences and bridges; irrigation systems; mowers, tractors and trucks; and roads and paths.

Sand and Top Dressing. The cost of sand and top dressing used on the golf course should be charged to this account.

Seeds, Flowers, and Shrubs. The cost of seeds, flowers, and shrubs used on the golf course should be charged to this account.

Small Tools. The cost of small tools such as races, shovels, etc. should be recorded in this account.

Telephone. Any telephone expenditures that can be directly related to the golf course maintenance department should be recorded in this account.

Topsoil. The cost of topsoil should be charged to this account.

Tree Care. The cost of maintaining trees on the golf course is recorded in this account. This also includes amounts paid to outsider contractors.

Uniforms. This item includes the cost or rental of uniforms for employees of the golf course maintenance department, as well as the cost of repairing uniforms of golf course maintenance department employees.

Vehicle Expense. The cost of operating and/or renting vehicles used by this department are recorded in this account.

Water. The cost of water purchased from outside sources for irrigating the golf course should be charged to this account.

Other Operating Expenses. This item includes costs of operating expenses applicable to the golf course maintenance department that do not apply to other line items discussed for this department.

ANALYSIS OF GOLF COURSE OPERATIONS

Considerable information is provided in the golf course operations schedule. Not only does it include detailed information by account classification, but generally the schedule will include both the monthly budget and actual figures, as well as the year-to-date budget and actual figures. The process of budgeting preparation and control is discussed in Chapter 7.

In order for this detailed information to be most useful to superintendents for management purposes, it must be analyzed. The analysis shown in this chapter will include five distinct methods:

1. horizontal analysis
2. vertical analysis
3. cost per hotel/round
4. base-year comparisons
5. ratio analysis

Each method will be explained and illustrated using the hypothetical Model Golf Club's course operations schedule. Exhibit 4.3 contains the Model Golf Club's golf course operations schedules for June over a three-year period. The schedule is abbreviated for illustrative purposes to simplify the discussion, and only a few expense classifications are shown. The concepts discussed may be applied to a more detailed schedule of an actual golf course enterprise.

	20X5	20X6	20X7
Payroll and Related Expenses			
Salaries and wages	$ 70,000	$ 72,500	$ 76,000
Payroll taxes and benefits	14,000	15,000	16,000
Total	84,000	87,500	92,000
Other Expenses			
Supplies	24,000	25,000	26,000
Repairs	11,000	12,000	13,000
Energy costs	5,000	4,000	6,000
Other	1,500	2,000	2,200
Total	41,500	43,000	47,200
Total Golf Course Maintenance Expenses	$125,500	$130,500	$139,200
Other Information			
Revenue from green fees	$ 60,000	$ 63,000	$ 68,000
Rounds of golf played	6,000	5,750	5,900

EXHIBIT 4.3. Golf Course Operations Schedule, Model Golf Club, for the month of June of 20X5–20X7

Horizontal Analysis

Horizontal analysis compares golf course operations schedules—generally the most recent month (or year) compared with the same month of the prior year. Alternatively, a comparison could be made to the prior month; however, due to the seasonal nature of most golf courses, a better comparison is with the same month of the prior year. The analysis includes the two sets of figures plus the changes between the two sets in both absolute and relative terms.

The absolute changes (dollar difference) reflect the change in dollars between the two months. For example, if salaries were $200,000 for 20X5 and $220,000 for 20X6, the absolute change is $20,000. The relative change (or percentage difference) is determined by dividing the absolute change ($20,000, as shown in the previous sentence) by the amount for the earliest period. Therefore, $20,000 divided by $200,000 equals 10 percent. The change in total salaries was $20,000, which is a 10 percent increase over the prior year. Superintendents must be able to explain any differences that their superiors would consider to be significant.

Exhibit 4.4 contains the horizontal analysis of the hypothetical Model Golf Club's schedule of golf course operations for June of 20X6 and 20X7. It

	20X6	20X7	Difference Dollar	Difference Percentage
Payroll and Related Expenses				
Salaries and wages	$ 72,500	$ 76,000	$3,500	4.8%
Payroll taxes and benefits	15,000	16,000	1,000	6.7
Total	87,500	92,000	4,500	5.1
Other Expenses				
Supplies	25,000	26,000	1,000	4.0
Repairs	12,000	13,000	1,000	8.3
Energy costs	4,000	6,000	2,000	50.0
Other	2,000	2,200	200	10.0
Total	43,000	47,200	4,200	9.8
Total Golf Course Maintenance Expenses	$130,500	$139,200	$8,700	6.7%

reflects both absolute and relative changes for each expense shown on the operations schedule. It is interesting to note that the largest increase—$3,500 for salaries and wages—is less than 5 percent of its base, while a $2,000 increase in energy costs is a 50 percent relative change. The club's green chairman and/or board of directors would most likely desire an explanation from the superintendent for the 50 percent increase in the use of energy during June 20X7 over June 20X6. Records of rainfall, average monthly temperatures, and so on would be useful in supporting the response.

Vertical Analysis

The second method for analyzing the golf course operations schedule is to reduce the numbers to percentages. This approach, called *vertical analysis*, is accomplished by having the total expense equal 100 percent and the individual cost categories equal percentages of 100 percent.

Vertical analysis of golf course operations permits a comparison of amounts relative to a base within each accounting period. Although horizontal analysis is restricted to internal use, vertical analysis comparisons can be made against the operating results of other golf enterprises. It might not be meaningful to compare the total salaries and wages of two different courses due to size; however, a realistic comparison could be made between salaries and wages as a percentage of total golf course maintenance expenses.

Assume that a relatively small enterprise has total salaries and wages for their golf course maintenance personnel of $80,000 for a year and a total expense budget of $160,000. Further, assume that a much larger club has a $300,000 labor cost against a total golf course maintenance expense of $550,000. The labor cost by percentage for the smaller operation is 50 percent while the labor cost percentage for the larger business is 54.6 percent. Although there may be many reasons to justify the difference of five percentage points, the simple illustration reflects the usefulness of this approach.

Exhibit 4.5 contains the vertical analysis for June of 20X6 and 20X7 of the hypothetical Model Golf Club's golf course operations. Notice that the analysis reflects two columns of amounts for June 20X6 and 20X7 and two columns of percentages for the same two months. The bottom line percentage is set at 100 percent and all individual amounts are a percentage of the total. For example, the 54.6 percent of salaries and wages for 20X7 was determined by dividing the salaries and wages of $76,000 for June 20X7 by the total expense of $139,200 for June 20X7.

All other percentages were determined in a similar fashion. There are some interesting but relatively minor differences. Even though salaries and

	20X6	20X7	20X6	20X7
Payroll and Related Expenses				
Salaries and wages	$ 72,500	$ 76,000	55.5%	54.6%
Payroll taxes and benefits	15,000	16,000	11.5	11.5
Total	87,500	92,000	67.0	66.1
Other Expenses				
Supplies	25,000	26,000	19.2	18.7
Repairs	12,000	13,000	9.2	8.3
Energy costs	4,000	6,000	3.1	4.3
Other	2,000	2,200	1.5	1.6
Total	43,000	47,200	33.0	33.9
Total Golf Course Maintenance Expenses	$130,500	$139,200	100.0%	100.0%

EXHIBIT 4.5. Vertical Analysis—Golf Course Operations Schedule, Model Golf Club, for the Month of June of 20X6–20X7

wages increased by $3,500 from June 20X6 to June 20X7—a 4.8 percent increase as shown by the horizontal analysis—salaries and wages as a percentage of the total expense have decreased from 55.5 percent to 54.6 percent. Energy costs is the other item to note, and this analysis shows an increase from 3.1 percent to 4.3 percent.

If the golf course operations schedule includes revenue, the total revenue is often set at 100 percent and all expenses percentages are calculated as a percentage of total revenue. Since the golf course operations department is generally considered to be a cost center, the above focus on total costs may be a more realistic and understandable presentation.

This analytical approach enables superintendents to gain greater insight into the cost structure and changes of their operation. They might find the analysis most useful in supporting future budget requests, especially where desired increases in a category appear to be significant by themselves but are reasonable when compared to the entire budget.

Cost per Hole

A third analytical approach to golf course operations is calculating the cost per unit of output and comparing the results to the prior period. Various useful units of measurement are the number of golf members, rounds played, and number of golf course holes. The calculation is conducted by dividing each expense account by the desired base number.

Exhibit 4.6 contains the cost per hole for our hypothetical Model Golf Club, which has an 18-hole course. Overall, the costs per hole for June 20X7 have increased by $483 over the costs per hole for the same month of the prior year. The cost per hole is shown for each expense line.

Golf industry cost figures published by PKF International in their annual publication, *Clubs in Town & Country*, are shown on a per hole basis. In a recent year, payroll costs were approximately $41,000 per hole on an annual basis, while other expenses were nearly $37,000, equaling an average golf course maintenance cost per hole of $78,000. Their publication showed an average cost per hole of approximately $16,000 20 years earlier. As with industry statistics, the numbers are strictly averages, not standards, and they result from the compilation of statistics from a wide range of golf clubs. The total average cost per hole of their study showed a range of approximately $68,000 per hole for clubs in the Eastern United States to over $95,000 per hole for clubs in the Western part of the United States. Exhibit 4.7 provides more detailed numbers. In addition, it reveals nonmaintenance golf expenses and golf income, resulting in *net golf expenses*.

	20X6	20X7	Difference
Payroll and Related Expenses			
Salaries and wages	$4,028	$4,222	$194
Payroll taxes and benefits	833	889	56
Total	4,861	5,111	250
Other Expenses			
Supplies	1,389	1,445	56
Repairs	667	722	55
Energy costs	222	333	111
Other	111	122	111
Total	2,389	2,622	233
Total Golf Course Maintenance Expense	$7,250	$7,733	$483

EXHIBIT 4.6. Golf Course Operations Cost Per Hole, Model Golf Club, for the Month of June 20X6 and 20X7

Average Cost per Hole, 2002	Geographic Divisions			
	All Country Clubs	East	Central	West
Payroll	$40,781	$37,818	$39,115	$45,390
Payroll taxes and benefits	8,394	6,853	6,367	11,306
Course supplies and contracts	9,134	8,734	8,987	9,720
Repairs and maintenance	3,644	4,716	1,546	3,177
Other costs	16,423	10,355	13,480	25,652
Total Golf Department Expenses	**$78,376**	**$68,476**	**$69,495**	**$95,245**
Less: Golf revenue	$38,359	$37,713	$41,177	$37,884
Net Golf Expenses	**$40,017**	**$30,713**	**$28,318**	**$57,361**

EXHIBIT 4.7. Golf Course Expenses Per Hole
Source: Clubs in Town & Country 2003 published by PKF International.

A superintendent might find these results useful for presenting to the enterprise's various committees and board as a means of information, especially when they compare favorably with industry averages.

Base Year Comparisons

A fourth analytical approach allows a meaningful comparison over several time periods. Using this approach, each amount for an account for the earliest time period is set equal to 100 percent, and corresponding amounts for future periods are determined as a percentage of the base period amount. For example, if salaries for an enterprise are $50,000, $55,000, $60,000, and $65,000 for four successive years, then their percentages for each of the four years would be 100 percent, 110 percent, 120 percent, and 130 percent. This shows that the salaries for the second year were 110 percent of the initial year's salaries, that salaries for the third year were 120 percent of the initial year's salaries, and so on.

Exhibit 4.8 contains an illustration of the base year comparison approach. Notice that each percentage for June 20X5 equals 100 percent. This analysis shows quite clearly how expenses have changed each year compared to the base period. One drawback of this approach is a small base period number, which might result in quite large percentages for future peri-

	20X5	20X6	20X7
Payroll and Related Expenses			
Salaries and wages	100.0%	103.6%	108.6%
Payroll taxes and benefits	100.0	107.1	114.3
Total	100.0	104.2	109.5
Other Expenses			
Supplies	100.0	104.2	108.3
Repairs	100.0	109.1	118.2
Energy costs	100.0	80.0	120.0
Other	100.0	133.3	146.7
Total	100.0	103.6	113.7
Total Golf Course Maintenance Expenses	100.0%	104.0%	110.9%

EXHIBIT 4.8. Base Year Comparison of the Golf Course Operations, Model Golf Club, for the Month of June of 20X5–20X7

ods. Therefore, if a base year number is unrealistically low or high, later results are abnormally impacted. This analysis provides useful results over several accounting periods. A superintendent might find this approach useful for reflecting changes over a five- to ten-year period to provide a perspective on changing costs of golf course maintenance.

Ratio Analysis

The final method of analysis is called ratio analysis. Only a brief discussion will be provided in this chapter, since Chapter 5 is devoted to this topic.

Ratio analysis results from comparing two or more related numbers to yield a single figure. Indeed, much of the analysis presented already is a form of ratio analysis. However, all of the focus thus far has been on the golf course operations schedule. With ratio analysis, one is not limited to a single schedule or financial statement but uses related numbers from various statements and schedules.

For example, a user of financial statements might want to know the cost of labor for the golf course operations as a percentage of the total labor cost of the enterprise. Another example of ratio analysis includes the calculation of green fees as a percentage of total golf course operations costs. A third example is the calculation of average green fees.

Two ratios of interest are as follows:

$$\text{Green fees to total golf course maintenance expenses} = \frac{\text{Green fees}}{\text{Total golf course maintenance expenses}}$$

This ratio reveals the percentage of maintenance costs covered by green fees.

$$\text{Average green fees} = \frac{\text{Total green fees}}{\text{Rounds of golf played}}$$

This ratio indicates the average green fee paid by golfers.

Both of these ratios are of interest in understanding golf revenues generated by the golf course, and when compared to the standard they reveal the degree of success in achieving revenue goals of the operation.

Using the information provided in Exhibit 4.3, the two ratios presented above are calculated for June of each year. The results are as follows:

	20X5	20X6	20X7
Green fees to total golf course maintenance expenses	47.8%	48.3%	48.9%

This ratio suggests that the Model Golf Club's green fees relative to its maintenance costs during the month of June are increasing for each year over the three-year period.

During 20X5, green fees were 47.8 percent of total golf course maintenance expenses, while by 20X7 the green fees were 48.9 percent. This indicates that green fees are rising faster than the maintenance expenses for the course.

	20X5	20X6	20X7
Average green fees	$10.00	$10.96	$11.53

The results reveal a fairly substantial increase in fees over the period of 20X5–20X7 for the month of June. Even though the rounds of golf played in June 20X7 were less than in June 20X6, revenue from fees was higher due to the increase in average green fees. Additional ratios will be presented and illustrated in the next chapter.

SUMMARY

The focus of the superintendent is maintenance of the golf course, which is shown in the golf course operations schedule of the enterprise's Income Statement. The schedule suggested by the Golf Course Association reflects both revenues and expenses. The expenses shown on this schedule are segregated into payroll and related expenses, and other expenses.

To gain the most information from the golf course operations schedule, the schedule should be analyzed. Five analytical methods are presented in this chapter. Although there is some overlap of these methods, each method provides additional insight useful to superintendents.

PROBLEMS

Problem 1

The Riverview Club's abbreviated golf course operations for 20X5 and 20X6 are as follows:

	20X5	20X6
Departmental Expenses		
Payroll and related expenses		
Salaries and wages	$180,000	$190,000
Payroll taxes and benefits	40,000	45,000
Total	220,000	235,000
Other Expenses		
Supplies	80,000	85,000
Repairs	25,000	22,000
Energy costs	20,000	22,000
Other	10,000	12,000
Total	135,000	141,000
Total Golf Course Maintenance Expenses	$355,000	$376,000

Required:
Conduct horizontal analysis of the Riverview Club's golf course operations schedule.

Problem 2

The Hilltop Golf Enterprise's golf course operations schedule for May 20X6 is as follows:

Hilltop Golf Enterprise
Golf Course Operations
For the month of May 20X6

Departmental Expenses	
Payroll and related expenses	
Salaries and wages	$20,000
Payroll taxes and employee benefits	5,000
Total payroll and related expenses	25,000
Other Expenses	
Ground and green supplies	
Fertilizer and topsoil	4,000
Insecticides	1,000
Gasoline and lubricants	300
Sand and cinders	200
Seeds, flowers, plants, and shrubs	2,000
Other supplies	300
Other operating expenses	900
Repairs Course buildings	500
Fences and bridges	200
Mowers, tractors, and trucks	3,500
Roads and paths	200
Water and drainage systems	1,800
Uniforms	200
Water and electricity	500
Total other expenses	15,600
Total Golf Course Maintenance Expenses	$40,600

Required:
Conduct vertical analysis of the Hilltop's golf course operations schedule for May 20X6.

MULTIPLE CHOICE QUESTIONS

1. Horizontal analysis reflects _____ between this month's operating numbers and the same month of the prior year.
   a. only dollar differences
   b. only percentage differences
   c. both dollar and percentage differences
   d. neither dollar nor percentage differences

2. A club's maintenance payroll for June 20X6 totaled $40,000 compared to $36,000 for June 20X5. The percentage difference is a _____.
   a. 10 percent increase
   b. 10 percent decrease
   c. 11.1 percent decrease
   d. 11.1 percent increase

3. Vertical analysis of an enterprise's course maintenance department is accomplished by converting the dollar amounts to percentages. _____ is set equal to 100 percent.
   a. Total payroll and related expenses
   b. Total other expenses
   c. Total golf course maintenance expenses
   d. Total enterprise expenses

4. Base year comparisons are conducted by
   a. setting total costs for each year equal to 100 percent.
   b. setting the amounts for each account for the earliest time period equal to 100 percent.
   c. setting total revenues for each year equal to 100 percent.
   d. the golf course's accountants once every five years.

5. The calculation of average green fees is an example of _____.
   a. ratio analysis
   b. vertical analysis
   c. horizontal analysis
   d. base year comparison

Analysis of Financial Statements

The financial statements of a golf course enterprise contain a great amount of information about the financial position and operations of a business. The balance sheet reflects assets, liabilities, and equity, while the income statement shows the revenues and expenses of the operation. Interpretation and greater understanding of these statements can be achieved by the financial analysis presented in this chapter.

The results of analysis are useful in several ways:

✦ **Purchasing a golf course.** When purchasing a golf course, it is crucial to analyze its past financial history, its current financial condition, and projected financial results. This will consist of performing tests on the historical financial records by using one or more of the ratios discussed in this chapter. It will also be important to apply the tests on the pro forma financial statements prepared for the future of the enterprise by using the same techniques.

For example, Joe has been approached by a group of investors who are seeking to buy an existing golf course, and want to make Joe an operating partner in the enterprise. Joe's salary would be paid in part with stock in the new enterprise. Joe needs to know whether the new club is financially viable, and he would use financial ratios to analyze the projected financial statements.

✦ **Starting a new enterprise.** When starting a new enterprise, it is crucial to make financial projections by describing the expected financial operations of the enterprise several years in the future. This will be an important test of its viability and will indicate whether the plans are realistic. The techniques discussed in this chapter will help in this effort.

Chris and several investors are thinking about starting a new golf course. Financial projections prepared include a pro forma income statement and balance sheet. Chris needs to determine whether the start-up proposal is sound before entering into the enterprise. Financial ratio analysis of the projected financial statements would give some indication about the financial health of the enterprise.

✦ **Managing the existing golf course.** As an operation moves into a rapid growth phase, or as it is managed on a regular basis, it is vital to monitor its financial well-being. This will help detect problems while they are still relatively minor. It will identify *lazy assets* that are consuming resources without providing sufficient return. It will also identify profit leaks—that is, excess or inappropriate expenses that rob the operation of its cash. It will further serve as the basis for making rational decisions about the transfer of assets, requirements for growth, and the effectiveness of efforts.

The owners of a hypothetical course are concerned about the reduced profitability of the course, and they question the ability of the superintendent. Financial ratio analysis can be performed to help pinpoint problem areas, and show just how well the superintendent is in fact performing his or her job for the course.

Financial analysis is accomplished by calculating ratios. Ratios simply are the comparison of two numbers. For example, depreciation expense divided by accounts receivable is a ratio, but to be meaningful the two numbers should be related. A common ratio computed by most operators is the *current ratio*, which is determined by dividing current assets by current liabilities. This ratio is meaningful in reflecting an operation's ability to pay its bills as they become due, since current liabilities reflect the enterprise's amount of bills due that will be paid with cash, which is part of current assets. Current assets also include other assets expected to be used in the enterprise or converted to cash in the near future.

Financial ratios are stated in terms of percentages (e.g., cost of labor percentage), in dollars (e.g., average green fee per round of golf), and in number of times (e.g., accounts receivable turnover). Regardless of how the ratio is stated, it must be compared to a standard. A course may have a current ratio of 2 to 1; however, that ratio is meaningless until it is compared with the *desired* current ratio, the current ratio for the prior period, or possibly even to an industry average. Generally, the most meaningful comparison is to the ratios computed from the budgeted numbers, since the budgeted amounts are the goals for this accounting period.

As good as ratios are in understanding the financials, they only provide insight. They do not solve the problem, as only management can resolve problems. For example, assume that the budgeted labor cost percentage for a hypothetical country club is 48 percent for June and the labor cost percentage for June was 50 percent. The calculated ratio suggests too much was expended on labor relative to sales; however, the causes at this point are unknown. Still, the comparison clearly indicates that it is an area of concern requiring additional study to determine the cause or causes of apparent excessive labor costs and follow-up management action to correct the problem.

CLASSES OF FINANCIAL RATIOS

Financial ratios may be classified by the type of information they provide. Financial ratios for golf course enterprises are divided into the five categories of liquidity, solvency, activity, profitability, and operations. Different users of financial statements—such as management, financial lenders, and owners tend to be interested in difference classes of ratios. Each class will be described, and the interest of the user groups will be briefly explained here; the rest of the chapter is devoted to explaining each ratio in more detail.

Liquidity Ratios

Liquidity ratios measure the enterprise's ability to meet its short-term obligations. Although the major focus of a golf course is providing services to its golfers, its bills must still be paid on a timely basis. The bills recorded as current liabilities are paid with cash from the operation. Current assets contain cash and other accounts that are expected to be converted into cash or used in the operation in the short run. Therefore, the focus of liquidity ratios is the current elements of a course's balance sheet. Management, especially the chief financial executive of the enterprise, must ensure that bills are paid on a timely basis. Other users of financial statements with a major interest in liquidity ratios include financial lenders.

Solvency Ratios

Solvency ratios measure the ability of the business to pay its bills in the long run. Two major subclasses of solvency ratios are computed—one from the balance sheet perspective and the other from the income statement. Financial lenders and owners are extremely interested in solvency ratios, since both of these financial statement users have long-term interest in the operation's finances.

Lenders want to be repaid their long-term loans, while profits accruing to owners might be paid only after all other claims are paid. The enterprise's top-level manager must keep both lenders and owners satisfied; thus, he or she wants solvency ratios to reflect reasonable financial risk. The golf course superintendents and other department heads generally direct their attention to the day-to-day activities, and leave this area of concern to others.

Profitability Ratios

Profitability ratios measure the golf course's ability to generate income for its owners. This is the major purpose, especially for profit-oriented courses. Therefore, to owners of such enterprises, these ratios are extremely important. A major concern of course owners is meeting the golfers' needs, and the profitability ratios are of reasonable interest, because today's profits must be reinvested in tomorrow's course improvements.

Others interested in profitability ratios include financial lenders and golf course managers and superintendents. Financial lenders are interested in these ratios because today's profits yield tomorrow's cash to make the course's future mortgage payments. Management is quite interested in these ratios because they also reflect management's overall performance. The golf course superintendent is interested in these ratios, as this period's profits are invested in future golf course improvements.

Activity Ratios

Activity ratios measure management's ability to use the assets entrusted to them. The assets entrusted to management are shown on the operation's balance sheet. The major asset for a golf course is usually the property and equipment. The use of these assets is often reflected by total revenues of the enterprise.

Everything else being equal, the greater the revenues, the greater the use of the course's assets. Generally, management has the most interest in activity ratios because they reflect management's ability to use resources. To a lesser extent, owners and financial leaders are also interested. However, the interest of those other than management increases only when the major financial goals of the enterprise are not realized.

Operating Ratios

Finally, operating ratios cover the operations (revenues and expenses) of the golf operation. There are an almost unlimited number of operating ratios of operations, including several for each profit, service, and cost center. A comparison of each expense to total expenses of a service center will yield a ratio for each expense category. However, a limited number of operating ratios are computed, and these focus on the major operating concerns of the enterprise.

For example, the food service department of a country club would generally be most concerned about sales, cost of food sold, and labor costs, and the three most common operating ratios in the food service area cover these three major aspects. For the golf course, considerable attention will be directed toward labor costs, since this is the major expense in maintaining the course.

As with activity ratios, management is most interested in these ratios, and the superintendent is most interested in financial ratios of the golf course maintenance department. Other users of financial statements, including financial lenders and owners, are interested in these ratios only as a backup to profitability ratios. In general, when the golf course enterprise is meeting the financial expectations of owners and lenders there is generally lessor concern about the details of operations.

A limited number of financial ratios will be presented and illustrated in the remainder of this chapter. The hypothetical Simple Club's abbreviated financial statements are limited to a balance sheet, income statement, and golf course operations schedule, as shown in Exhibits 5.1, 5.2, and 5.3.

TYPES OF LIQUIDITY RATIOS

Current Ratios

The *current ratio* measures an enterprise's ability to pay its bills as they become due. The current ratio is as follows:

$$\text{Current ratio:} \quad \frac{\text{Current assets}}{\text{Current liabilities}}$$

	20X5	20X6
Current Assets		
Cash	$ 10,000	$ 12,000
Accounts receivable	60,000	65,000
Inventories	10,000	8,000
Prepaid expenses	7,000	6,000
Total current assets	87,000	91,000
Investments	100,000	200,000
Property and Equipment		
Land and land improvements	800,000	800,000
Buildings and building improvements	2,000,000	2,000,000
Furniture and equipment	700,000	800,000
Less: accumulated depreciation and amortization	<2,000,000>	<2,100,000>
Net property equipment	1,500,000	1,500,000
Total Assets	$1,687,000	$1,791,000
Current Liabilities		
Accounts payable	$20,000	$ 15,000
Taxes payable	7,000	6,000
Accrued wages	4,000	4,000
Current portion of long-term debt	20,000	20,000
Total current liabilities	51,000	45,000
Long-Term Liabilities		
Mortgage payable	500,000	580,000
Less portion due within one year	<20,000>	<20,000>
Total long-term liabilities	480,000	560,000
Total Liabilities	531,000	605,000
Owners' Equity		
Capital stock	1,000,000	1,000,000
Retained earnings	156,000	186,000
Total owners' equity	1,156,000	1,186,000
Total Liabilities and Owners' Equity	$1,687,000	$1,791,000

EXHIBIT 5.1. Simple Club Balance Sheet for the Years 20X5 and 20X6

Departmental and Sports Revenue	
Golf course operations	$ 600,000
Car rentals	50,000
Food and beverage	400,000
Other income	30,000
Total revenue	1,080,000
Departmental and Sports Expenses	
Golf course operations	400,000
Car rentals	40,000
Food and beverage	250,000
Total costs and expenses	690,000
Income before Undistributed Operating Expenses	390,000
Undistributed Operating Expenses	
Administrative and general	70,000
Advertising and sales promotion	30,000
Heat, light, and power	20,000
Repairs and maintenance	50,000
Total undistributed operating expenses	170,000
Gross operating profit before fixed charges	220,000
Fixed Charges	
Insurance—fire and general liability	10,000
Rent and property taxes	30,000
Interest expense	30,000
Total fixed charges	70,000
Income Before Provision for Depreciation	150,000
Depreciation Expense	100,000
Income Before Income Taxes	50,000
Income Taxes	20,000
Net Income	$ 30,000

EXHIBIT 5.2. Simple Club Statement of Income and Expense for the Year 20X6

Revenue	
Daily green fees	$400,000
Annual green fees	200,000
Total Revenue	600,000
Departmental Expenses	
Payroll and related expenses:	
Salaries and wages	160,000
Payroll taxes and employee benefits	40,000
Total payroll and related expenses	200,000
Other Expenses:	
Supplies	50,000
Repairs	100,000
Energy costs	40,000
Other	10,000
Total other expenses	200,000
Total Departmental Expenses	400,000
Golf Course Operations Income	$200,000

EXHIBIT 5.3. Simple Club Golf Course Operations Schedule for the Year 20X6. This schedule has been summarized to simplify the presentation.

Both current assets and current liabilities are shown on the enterprise's balance sheet. The current ratio for the Simple Club at the end of 20X6 is just over 2.

$$\frac{\text{Current assets}}{\text{Current liabilities}} = \frac{\$91,000}{\$45,000} = 2.02$$

Thus, for each $1 of current liabilities at the end of 20X6, the Simple Club has $2.02 of current assets. Is this an acceptable liquidity position? One must compare this to its past liquidity levels and its liquidity objective. The Simple Club's current ratio at the end of 20X5 was 1.71, determined by dividing the current assets of $87,000 by current liabilities of $51,000. Thus, the current ratio of 2.02 is a considerable improvement in liquidity. Still, it should be compared with the club's objective for this area.

Accounts Receivable Turnover

A second liquidity ratio is the *accounts receivable turnover*. This ratio measures the club's ability to convert its receivables into cash, and it is determined as follows:

$$\text{Accounts receivable turnover} = \frac{\text{Revenues}}{\text{Average accounts receivable}}$$

The revenues in the formula are taken from the enterprise's income statement, which covers one year in our illustration. The accounts receivable numbers are from the Balance Sheet, a statement reflecting the financial position at only one point in time. This formula requires that an average of the accounts receivable be used, which is determined by summing the accounts receivable at the beginning and end of 20X6 and dividing the sum by two. The average accounts receivable for the Simple Club is $62,500 and the accounts receivable turnover is 17.28 times, determined as follows:

$$\frac{\text{Revenues}}{\text{Average accounts receivable}} = \frac{\$1,080,000}{\$62,500} = \underline{\underline{17.28 \text{ times}}}$$

This result reveals that the average receivables were turned over 17 times, or in terms of number of days, every 21 days (365 days/year divided by 17.28 = 21.12 days). As with other financial ratios, the result must be compared against the golf course enterprise's standard to determine its significance.

TYPES OF SOLVENCY RATIOS

Two solvency ratios are presented in this chapter to indicate the extent to which the enterprise is operating on borrowed funds and to indicate its ability to pay its bills over the long term. These ratios are the debt/equity ratio and the number of times interest earned ratio.

Debt/Equity Ratio

The *debt/equity ratio* compares the total liabilities of the enterprise with the total owners' equity. Both of these numbers are taken from the enterprise's balance sheet. In general, the greater the debt relative to equity, the greater the finance leverage. Although this can result in excellent financial returns for a very successful golf operation, there is also greater financial risk, since the debt must be repaid in the future. The debt/equity ratio is computed as follows:

$$\text{Debt/equity ratio} = \frac{\text{Total liabilities}}{\text{Total owners' equity}}$$

The debt/equity ratio of the Simple Club is 51.01% at the end of 20X6, computed as follows:

$$\frac{\text{Total liabilities}}{\text{Total owners' equity}} = \frac{\$605,000}{\$1,186,000} = \underline{\underline{51.01\%}}$$

This suggests that the Simple Club has one dollar of equity for every $0.51 it owes. Compared to the beginning of the year when its debit/equity ratio was 45.93 percent, this reflects an increase in leverage or relatively greater financial risk for owners of the Simple Club. Again, the major question to be answered is, "What is the objective in this area?" If the funds borrowed during 20X6 can generate future returns in excess of the cost of the funds (interest), then the borrowing is generally considered not only acceptable but also desirable.

Number of Times Interest Earned Ratio

The second solvency ratio—*number of times interest earned*—focuses on an enterprise's ability to make its interest payments. In general, the higher the ratio, the lower the risk. The number of times interest earned ratio is calculated as follows:

$$\text{Number of times interest earned} = \frac{\text{Income before interest expense and taxes}}{\text{Interest expense}}$$

The numbers used in this ratio come from the Income Statement, thus reflecting an enterprise's debt-paying ability over a period of time. The number of times interest earned ratio for the Simple Club for 20X6 is 2.67 times, determined as follows:

$$\frac{\text{Income before interest expense and taxes}}{\text{Interest expense}} = \frac{\$80,000}{\$30,000} = \underline{\underline{2.67}} \text{ times}$$

where income before interest expense and income taxes is determined by adding up net income + income taxes + interest expense (i.e., 30,000 + 20,000 + 30,000 = 80,000).

A common use of this ratio is to compare the same ratio computed for the prior year to the desired results.

TYPES OF PROFITABILITY RATIOS

The profitability ratios presented in this book include profit margin, return on assets, and return on owners' equity. As discussed previously, the owners of a course, especially a profit-oriented course, are most interested in these ratios.

Profit Margin

The *profit margin ratio* compares the bottom-line operating results—that is, net income—to the total revenue of the enterprise. The formula for this ratio is as follows:

$$\text{Profit margin ratio} = \frac{\text{Net income}}{\text{Total revenues}}$$

This ratio is an overall measure of what percentage of revenue results in profit. The higher the percentage, the greater is management's ability to operate the enterprise.

For the Simple Club, the profit margin ratio was 2.78 percent for 20X6. The ratio was computed as follows:

$$\frac{\text{Net income}}{\text{Total revenues}} = \frac{\$30,000}{\$1,080,000} = 2.78\%$$

Common comparisons would be made to the prior years—most importantly, to the enterprise's goal for the year, as shown in the operating budget.

Return on Assets

A second profitability ratio is *return on assets*. This ratio compares the net income for the period with the average total assets. As with the accounts receivable turnover, since the numerator of the ratio (net income) is for a period of time, then an average of the total assets must be used. The formula is as follows:

$$\text{Return on total assets} = \frac{\text{Net income}}{\text{Average total assets}}$$

The higher the return, the greater is the profitability from using the assets. For the Simple Club, the average total assets are calculated as follows:

Beginning of 20X6	$1,687,000
End of 20X6	1,791,000
Total	$3,478,000
Divided by two:	÷2
Average total assets	$1,739,000

The club's return on total assets is 1.73 percent, determined as follows:

$$\frac{\text{Net income}}{\text{Average total assets}} = \frac{\$30,000}{\$1,739,000} = 1.73\%$$

The return on assets for 20X6 is 1.73 percent, which must be compared to the prior years and the enterprise's objective in order to determine its relevance.

Return on Owners' Equity

The third profitability ratio is *return on owners' equity*. This ratio compares the profits of the course to the equity of the owners in the enterprise. The formula is as follows:

$$\text{Return on owners' equity} = \frac{\text{Net income}}{\text{Average owners' equity}}$$

As with any investment, owners desire a high return. However, if a high return is achieved at the expense of quality of the enterprise's golfing and other activities, at best this will probably only be a short-term result. On the other hand, a low return does not guarantee excellence, either. The results achieved, as with other ratios, must be compared with past results and the goal for the current accounting period.

The Simple Club's return on owners' equity for 20X6 is 2.56 percent, calculated as follows:

$$\frac{\text{Net income}}{\text{Average owners' equity}} = \frac{\$30,000}{\$1,171,000} = 2.56\%$$

As with the prior ratio, the denominator of this ratio uses an average that is based on numbers for the beginning and end of the year for the Simple Club.

TYPES OF ACTIVITY RATIOS

Two activity ratios are presented and illustrated in this chapter. These ratios reflect the use of resources by management. The two ratios are the property and equipment turnover and the total assets turnover. Each ratio considers the revenues of the enterprise, as shown on the income statement, and the value of resources, as shown on the balance sheet. Generally speaking, the higher the turnover results, the greater the utilization of the assets.

Property and Equipment Turnover

The property and equipment turnover is determined as follows:

$$\text{Property and equipment turnover} = \frac{\text{Total revenues}}{\text{Average property and equipment}}$$

For the Simple Club, this ratio is 0.72 times for 20X6. The calculation is as follows:

$$\frac{\text{Total revenues}}{\text{Average property and equipment}} = \frac{\$1,080,000}{\$1,500,000} = 0.72 \text{ times}$$

The result suggests that for each $1.00 of property and equipment $0.72 in revenues was generated. Common comparisons of this result would be to the prior periods and the targeted ratio for the year.

Total Asset Turnover

The *total asset turnover* is calculated as follows:

$$\text{Total asset turnover} = \frac{\text{Total revenues}}{\text{Average total assets}}$$

As with the property and equipment turnover ratio, the higher the ratio the better, because a high turnover suggests a greater use of the assets than a lower turnover.

$$\frac{\text{Total revenues}}{\text{Average total assets}} = \frac{\$1,080,000}{\$1,739,000} = 0.621 \text{ times}$$

An interesting combination of this ratio and the profit margin ratio (a profitability ratio) yields the return on total assets (also a profitability ratio) as follows:

Profit margin ratio × Total assets turnover = Return on total assets

For the Simple Club the result is as follows:

$$2.78\% \times 0.621 = \underline{1.73\%}$$

TYPES OF OPERATING RATIOS

There are many operating ratios for each area of activity of the enterprise. Common operating ratios for food and beverage would include average food service check, labor cost percentage, and cost of food sold percentage.

For many golf course enterprises, the focus of the superintendent is the maintenance of the golf course, and the superintendent has little or no direct responsibility or control over golf course revenues; however, since golfers will be affected by the quality of the course, the golf course superintendent has a very strong indirect influence on revenues. In the prior chapter, two operating ratios for golf course operations departments were presented. Additional ratios include each expense as a percentage of the total expenses of the department, and—for enterprises that show golfing revenues on the golf course operations schedule—ratios reflecting the percentage of each expense to total revenues.

The Simple Club operating results for the golf course will be used to illustrate several operating ratios, as follows:

Ratio	Formula	Calculation	
Labor cost %	Total payroll and related exp. / Total revenues	$\dfrac{\$200{,}000}{\$600{,}000}$	$= \underline{\underline{33.33\%}}$
Other expenses %	Total other expenses / Total revenues	$\dfrac{\$200{,}000}{\$600{,}000}$	$= \underline{\underline{33.33\%}}$
Labor cost %	Total payroll and related exp. / Total departmental expenses	$\dfrac{\$200{,}000}{\$400{,}000}$	$= \underline{\underline{50\%}}$
Energy cost %	Energy costs / Total revenues	$\dfrac{\$40{,}000}{\$600{,}000}$	$= \underline{\underline{6.67\%}}$

The meaning of each ratio is self-explanatory, and several more ratios could be calculated. The meaningfulness of the ratios is achieved by comparing the results to past ratios and to ratios from the budget figures for the accounting period.

Operating ratios are illustrated for the golf course operations department only; however, as stated before, similar analysis should be conducted for each activity area of the enterprise. Since the golf course superintendent's responsibility is for maintaining the course, he/she will use the operating ratios most frequently. Those ratios applied to the golf course maintenance expenses should enable the superintendent to better manage operations. The ratios for the enterprise as a whole and other profit and cost centers provide the superintendent with a better understanding of the entire operation.

SUMMARY

Financial analysis is useful for gaining understanding of an enterprise's financial statements. Five classes of ratios include liquidity, solvency, profitability, activity, and operations. Various users of financial statements have different levels of interest in financial ratios, depending on their interest in the golf course enterprise.

Two or three ratios are presented and illustrated in this chapter for each class of ratios using the hypothetical Simple Club. Each ratio provides meaning when it is compared to a standard, which often includes the same ratios for the prior accounting period and the targeted ratio based on the operations budget.

PROBLEMS

Problem 1

The Leaping Deer Golf Course's abbreviated Balance Sheet and Income Statement are shown below.

**Balance Sheet
(in thousands)**

	20X5	20X6
Current Assets	$ 50	$ 60
Investments	100	140
Property and Equipment	2,850	2,900
Total Assets	$3,000	$3,100
Current Liabilities	$ 30	$ 35
Long-Term Liabilities	1,000	950
Owners' Equity	1,970	2,115
Total Liability and Owners' Equity	$3,000	$3,100

**Income Statement
(in thousands)**

20X6	
Total Revenues	$1,500
Total Departmental Costs	900
Undistributed Operating Expenses	300
Gross Operating Profit Before Fixed Charges	300
Fixed Charges	100
Depreciation	100
Income Taxes	40
Net Income	$ 60

Required: Calculate the following ratios:
1. Current ratio for 20X6
2. Debt/equity ratio for 20X6
3. Profit margin ratio
4. Return on total assets
5. Return on owners' equity

Problem 2

Several ratios for a four-year period of the Oakview Club are as follows:

	20X3	20X4	20X5	20X6
Current Ratio	1.4	1.45	1.5	1.55
Accounts Receivable Turnover	20	19	18	17
Return on Total Assets	2%	2.5%	3%	3.5%
Profit Margin Ratio	3%	3.5%	3.5%	4%
Return of Owners' Equity	4%	3.5%	3%	2.5%

Required:

1. Comment on the club's change in liquidity over the four-year period.
2. Comment on the club's changing profitability over the four-year period.

MULTIPLE CHOICE QUESTIONS

1. The major purpose in calculating financial ratios is:
   a. they solve problems encountered by the operation.
   b. they are challenging and enjoyable to work.
   c. they provide insight in understanding the financial statements.
   d. all of the above.

2. _____ ratios measure the enterprise's ability to meet its short-term obligations.
   a. Liquidity
   b. Solvency
   c. Profitability
   d. Activity

3. Once an operating ratio is computed, it should be compared to a standard. The best standard is probably the ratio based on _____.
   a. the prior month
   b. the prior year
   c. the financial plan for the accounting period
   d. industry averages

Data for questions 4 and 5 are as follows:

XYZ Club
Summarized Balance Sheet
December 31, 20X6

Assets	
Current assets	$ 100,000
Noncurrent assets	1,900,000
Total Assets	$2,000,000
Liabilities and Owners' Equity	
Liabilities:	
Current liabilities	$ 80,000
Long-term debt	920,000
Total Liabilities	$1,000,000
Owners' Equity:	$1,000,000
Total Liabilities and Owners' Equity	$2,000,000

4. The current ratio of the XYZ Club is _____.
   a. 2 to 1
   b. 1.25 to 1
   c. 1 to 1
   d. 0.8 to 1

5. The debt/equity ratio of the XYZ Club is _____.
   a. 1 to 1
   b. 0.8 to 1
   c. 0.5 to 1
   d. 0.25 to 1

Breakeven Analysis

The manager of every golf course operation would like to be able to predict the bottom-line (net income or loss) results of his/her operation prior to the production of the financial statements. Breakeven analysis is a tool that, when properly used, will allow a reasonably accurate prediction of the profits of an enterprise for the accounting period. Even though this tool is often referred to as *breakeven analysis*, a broader term is *cost-volume-profit analysis*. In essence, the breakeven point (revenues equaling expenses) is but one point on a continuum of possible operating outcomes for a business.

This tool will enable the golf course superintendent to better understand the relationship among revenues, expenses, levels of activity, and profitability. The major objective of many golfing enterprises may not be earning profits; still, the profit motivation is high even for nonprofit organizations, since today's profits yield future cash flows for maintaining and even enhancing a golf course's facilities and operations.

This chapter will start with the definition and illustration of types of costs. Next, the basic formula for breakeven analysis is provided, along with an illustration. Third, various targeted profitability levels are introduced into the equation, along with income taxes. Finally, the breakeven analysis concepts will be applied to special projects.

TYPES OF COSTS

The expenses of a golf enterprise, referred to as costs, may be understood based on how they change as the activity of the golf course changes. That is, costs may be viewed as fixed, variable, or mixed (partly fixed and partly variable).

Fixed costs are those that remain constant in the short run (time period of one year or less) even though the activity of the course increases or decreases. An example of a fixed cost is the salary of the course superintendent. In general, within the short run—whether course activity increases or decreases—the periodic (weekly, biweekly, semimonthly or monthly) salary remains constant. The graph in Exhibit 6.1 reflects the nature of fixed costs in relation to activity. Costs are shown on the vertical axis, while activity is plotted on the horizontal axis.

Although fixed costs are constant in the short run, all fixed costs change over longer periods of time. For example, salaries are increased, and depreciation (generally considered to be a fixed cost) increases as more equipment is purchased.

Variable costs change proportionally with the volume of activity. As a course is played more frequently, more costs are incurred. For example, consider a course that requires players to use golf cars. Assume that after each round of golf is played, the batteries must be charged, at an estimated cost of $0.50. In this case, the electricity related to the golf cars is a variable expense, since the greater the rounds of golf played, the greater the use of cars; thus the greater the electricity usage.

Another example of a variable expense would be the cost of golf attire sold and food and beverages consumed. Though not every golfer will purchase golf attire or even food or beverages, the more golfers there are, the greater the increase in sales in these areas; thus the greater the increase in variable expenses.

EXHIBIT 6.1. Graphical Depiction of Fixed Costs

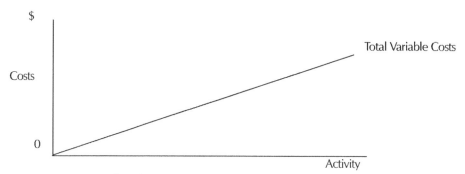

EXHIBIT 6.2. Graphical Depiction of Variable Costs

The graph in Exhibit 6.2 shows the relationship between variable costs and volume of activity. When activity is zero (no golf is played during the day; the course is closed), then variable costs are zero. Further, as the rounds of golf increase, the variable costs increase.

The third type of cost is the mixed cost. This cost consists of both fixed and variable costs, that is, a portion of the mixed cost is fixed and a portion is variable. Consider the hourly labor required to maintain a golf course. The higher the rounds of golf played, the greater the hours to maintain the course. A certain amount of hourly labor is required to mow the course and perform other maintenance tasks regardless of the number of rounds played. However, other maintenance, such as repairing divots, increases directly with the increase in rounds played. Another example would be telephone expense. Even when the telephone is not used, the telephone company charges a fixed fee for the system. As the activity of the course increases, telephone usage increases, and the increased cost is the variable portion of the total telephone expense.

Exhibit 6.3 depicts a mixed cost. Notice that a portion of the expense is fixed and a portion is variable. The two portions combined equal the total mixed costs. When the enterprise's activity is at zero, then the fixed cost portion of the mixed costs is the only cost incurred.

The mixed costs can be separated into their fixed and variable portions and combined with other fixed and variable costs for breakeven analysis. Exhibit 6.4 depicts the total theoretical costs of a golf course.

The total costs of a golf course can be determined using the following equation.

$$TC = \text{fixed costs} + (\text{variable cost per round} \times \text{number of rounds})$$

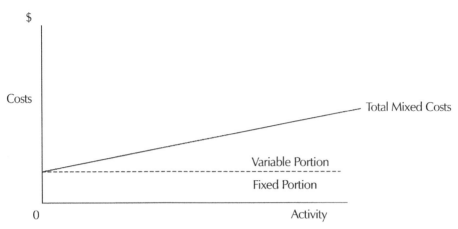

EXHIBIT 6.3. Graphical Depiction of Total Mixed Costs

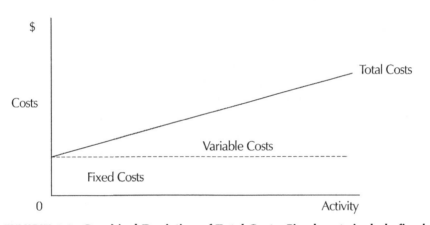

EXHIBIT 6.4. Graphical Depiction of Total Costs. Fixed costs include fixed costs and the fixed portion of mixed costs. Variable costs include variable costs and the variable portion of mixed costs.

An estimation of the TC for the hypothetical Highland Golf Course (HGC) for the month of June when 10,000 rounds of golf are played and the fixed costs are $60,000 and variable costs are $2.00 per round is $80,000.

$$TC = \$60,000 + (\$2 \times 10,000)$$

$$TC = \underline{\$80,000}$$

Given the TC equation for the HGC, the estimate of TC when 12,000 rounds are played would be $84,000. The difference between total costs for

10,000 rounds and total costs for 12,000 rounds is $4,000. This difference is simply the difference in rounds multiplied by the variable cost per round of $2. Fixed costs, as defined in this chapter, do not change in the short run, such as when the golf activity increases from 10,000 rounds to 12,000 rounds.

Now, let's consider the breakeven model. Since costs have been covered as well as different levels of activity, only revenue must be added.

BREAKEVEN ANALYSIS

The equation to determine breakeven for an enterprise offering only golf services is as follows:

$$X = \frac{F}{S - V}$$

where X = rounds of golf as breakeven
      F = total fixed costs for the accounting period
      S = average greens fees
      V = variable cost per round of golf

Remember, at the breakeven point the course's total revenue exactly equals the course's total costs, resulting in a bottom line of zero.

Exhibit 6.5 is a graphical depiction of the breakeven point of a golf course. This graph includes a fixed cost line for the accounting period, a total costs line, and a total revenue line. When the golfing activity is zero for the accounting period, the bottom-line operating result is a net loss equal to the fixed costs.

The intersection of the total costs and total revenue lines is the breakeven point. To the left of the breakeven point a loss is shown, while to the right of the breakeven point a profit is shown. The amount of the profit for the operation, as depicted on this graph, is the vertical distance between the total revenue and total costs lines to the right of the breakeven point.

Consider the hypothetical Sunshine Golf Course (SGC), which is a daily fee course. Each round of golf costs $25, and the total monthly fixed costs equal $88,000, while the variable costs per round played are $3.00. Given the cost structure of the SGC, the breakeven point is 4,000 rounds of golf.

$$X = \frac{\$88,000}{\$25 - \$3}$$

$$X = \frac{\$88,000}{\$22} = \$4,000$$

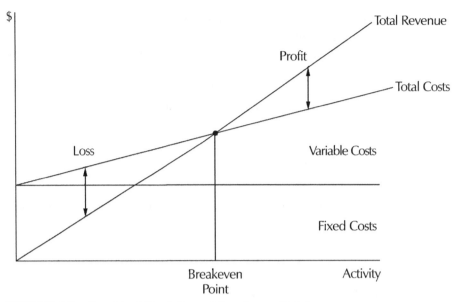

EXHIBIT 6.5. Graphical Depiction of Breakeven Point

The proof of this calculation is as follows:

Greens fees (4,000 × $25)	$100,000
Variable costs (4,000 × $3)	12,000
Fixed costs	88,000
Net income	$ 0

The breakeven analysis reveals that the SGC will break even during the month when 4,000 rounds of golf are played. However, who really wants to just break even?

In order to determine the level of activity required to generate a desired profit, the breakeven formula must be modified by adding the amount of desired profit to the numerator of the equation, as follows:

$$\text{Rounds of golf} = \frac{P+F}{S-V}$$

where P stands for desired profit.

To illustrate this formula, which provides the desired rounds of play given a desired profit level, the SGC example is used again. Assume the SGC wants to make a profit of $11,000 during the month of June. How many rounds must be played? Since rounds at breakeven equaled 4,000, we know the required rounds must be greater than 4,000.

The answer is calculated as follows:

$$X = \frac{\$11,000 + \$88,000}{\$25 - \$3}$$

$$X = \frac{\$99,000}{\$22} = 4,500 \text{ rounds}$$

When 4,500 rounds are played at SGC during June, $11,000 of profit is earned. Thus, the level of activity required to earn the $11,000 is 500 rounds above breakeven. The required rounds *above breakeven* could also be determined by simply dividing the desired profit by the difference between the greens fees and the variable costs per round, as follows:

$$\text{Required rounds above breakeven} = \frac{P}{S - X}$$

$$= \frac{\$11,000}{\$22}$$

$$= \underline{\underline{500}} \text{ rounds}$$

If the hypothetical SGC could lower its variable costs by $1 per round from $3 to $2, then the breakeven would be lowered, as follows:

$$X = \frac{\$88,000}{\$25 - \$2} = 3,826.1 \text{ rounds}$$

Likewise, if the SGC lowered its monthly fixed costs by $10,000 from $88,000 to $78,000, the breakeven point would also be lowered, as follows:

$$X = \frac{\$78,000}{\$25 - \$3} = 3,545.5 \text{ rounds}$$

However, with the lowering of costs the quality of play most likely would be lessened, perhaps resulting in fewer rounds of golf. Therefore, the course superintendent must be extremely cautious about making cost cuts without carefully considering the overall impact on course operations.

If the SGC is able to increase its average greens fees while holding monthly fixed costs at $88,000 and variable costs at $3 per round, the breakeven point is reduced. Consider a $1 increase from $25 per round to $26. The revised breakeven point is as follows:

$$X = \frac{\$88,000}{\$26 - \$3} = 3{,}826.1 \text{ rounds}$$

Notice the breakeven point is the same—3,826.1 rounds—as that of the unilateral reduction of variable costs from $3 to $2 per round shown above. The reason for this is that under both scenarios the difference between the greens fees and variable costs per round is $23.

Breakeven analysis is further complicated when a person considers federal income taxes and the fact that golf course operations include other profit centers, such as pro shops and food and beverage outlets. These more complicated situations are beyond the scope of this book![1]

SPECIAL PROJECTS

The concepts of fixed and variable costs and breakeven analysis may also be applied to special projects. For example, a golf course superintendent might want to increase the rounds played by having forward tees installed on the golf course. The manager and the board of directors of the course may be resistant to this proposal unless it can be shown to be profitable.

The analysis to support this proposal should consider the *additional* revenue to be generated by the increase in rounds of golf related to the forward tees, as well as the increases in costs, including both fixed and variable costs.

The analysis would include a modification of the breakeven formula, as follows:

$$X = \frac{C}{S - V}$$

where C = cost of the project
          S = greens fees per round
          V = variable costs per round
          X = breakeven point in rounds

To illustrate the use of this formula, the hypothetical SGC example is used. Assume the SGC has forward tees installed on its course at a cost of

---

[1] The reader interested in more complicated cases should consider reading the coverage of C-V-P analysis in the author's text, *Hospitality Industry Managerial Accounting*, 5th Edition (Lansing, Mich.: The Educational Institute of the AH&LA).

$110,000. How many rounds of golf must be played in order for the enterprise to recover the installation costs?

$$X = \frac{\$110,000}{\$25 - \$3}$$

$$X = \frac{\$110,000}{\$22} = 5,000 \text{ rounds}$$

The answer of 5,000 rounds means that 5,000 rounds must be played in order for the GSC to earn profits equal to the installation costs. This simplified example assumes all rounds related to the forward tees are additional rounds; thus they are not displacing rounds that would have been played anyway. Further, it assumes there are no additional fixed costs beyond the cost of installing the forward tees.

Further consideration of this illustration could include the time requirement. If an average of 50 rounds can be played per day from GSC's newly installed forward tees, then 100 golfing days are required to break even on this proposed project:

$$\frac{\text{Required rounds}}{\text{Rounds per day}} = \frac{5,000}{50} = 100 \text{ days}$$

SUMMARY

Breakeven analysis reveals the level of activity required at a golf course in order for the course's bottom line for the period to be zero. For an enterprise offering only golfing services, this is determined by dividing the fixed costs for the accounting period by the difference between greens fees per round and variable costs per round. In addition, the volume of golfing activity required to earn a profit is determined by modifying the breakeven equation. The desired profit is simply added to the total fixed costs, which is then divided by the difference between revenue and variable costs per round.

This analytical approach can also be used to determine either the breakeven or any level of profitability for special projects. In addition, "what-if" scenarios can be explored by varying one element of the breakeven equation and recalculating X Although this tool is useful for understanding the dynamics of the interrelationship of costs, revenues, and volume, changes in costs and fees should be undertaken only after fully considering all facets of the golf course operation.

PROBLEMS

Problem 1

The proposed Fairview Golf Course (FGC) is a pay-for-play course. The feasibility study suggests greens fees of $12. Analysis of the cost structure of the FGC reveals monthly fixed costs of $60,000 and variable costs of $2 per round.

Required:

1. How many rounds must be played during a month to break even?
2. How many rounds must be played during the year to break even? Assume that due to adverse weather the course is open only nine months of the year, but that monthly fixed costs are $60,000 whether the course is open or not.
3. How many rounds must be played during the year if $50,000 in profit is to be realized?

Problem 2

Assume the Westside Golf Course proposes to acquire golf cars. The cost of the cars, course modifications for the cars, and a building to house the cars is estimated to be $160,000. The expected charge per cart is $6 per round, and variable costs per car per round are estimated to be $2.

Required:

1. How many car rentals are required in order to break even on this project?
2. If the average car rentals per day is 100, how long will it take for the course to reach breakeven on this project?

MULTIPLE CHOICE QUESTIONS

1. A _____ cost remains constant in relation to the changes in revenue in the short run.
   a. fixed
   b. variable
   c. mixed
   d. none of the above

2. Theoretically, when revenue is zero (during a month the golf enterprise is closed) _____ expenses are zero.
   a. fixed
   b. variable
   c. mixed
   d. none of the above

3. The breakeven point for an enterprise is when
   a. revenues exceed expenses
   b. expenses exceed revenues
   c. expenses equal revenues
   d. none of the above

4. The Spartan Golf Course is a pay-for-play operation. Its average monthly fixed costs are $50,000; its average greens fee is $12.00 per round; and its average variable cost per round is $2.00. The breakeven point (in rounds) during a month is _____ rounds.
   a. 25,000
   b. 5,000
   c. 4,167
   d. none of the above

5. Assume that the Spartan Golf Course (mentioned in Question 4) wants to earn $10,000 in profits during a month. How many rounds of golf must be played on a monthly basis *in excess* of its breakeven?
   a. 10,000
   b. 9,167
   c. 5,000
   d. 1,000
   e. none of the above

7

Operating Budgets

Every rational manager plans for the future. Some plans are formalized—that is, they are written—while others remain informal. Budgets are written plans reduced to dollars, generally for a period of time. They provide answers to many questions of the golf course's executive staff, such as the following:

1. What are the forecasted greens fees for the month?
2. What is the budgeted golf course labor cost for the year?
3. What is the estimated depreciation for the period?
4. How close was the actual labor expense to the budget for the last month?
5. What is the projected bottom line for the golf course for the year?

This chapter focuses on operating budgets. It covers types of budgets, purposes of budgeting, the budget preparation process, and budgetary control.

TYPES OF BUDGETS

Golf course executives prepare several types of budgets. The operating budget, also referred to as the income and expense budget, includes the enterprise's plans for generating revenues and incurring expenses for a given period of time. Generally, monthly budgets are prepared, and the sum of the 12 monthly budgets constitutes the annual operating budget. The operating budget includes the detailed schedule of revenue and expenses for the golf course. For many courses, the budget for the golf course superintendent is limited to the expense categories for his/her department. The operations budget enables the superintendent and other management executives to accomplish two of its major functions: planning and control.

Two other types of budgets are capital improvements budgets and cash budgets. The cash budget shows the projected cash receipts and disbursements for the course. The difference in time between the generation of revenues and the related cash receipt can be substantial for golf operations such as country clubs. Country club members are billed for services for one month and generally are not expected to pay until the next month. The cash budget enables the club's financial executives to track and control cash. The capital improvements budget is the topic of the next chapter of this book. This budget's focus is the acquisition of equipment and facilities. The course superintendent needs to thoroughly understand this process because (1) their equipment needs are extensive, and (2) capital budgeting approaches presented in this book, when properly used, should enable superintendents to cost justify their capital needs.

PURPOSES OF BUDGETING

Many small golf operations have been slow to formalize their operating budgets. Often the overall goals, revenues, expense operations—and the desired bottom line—remain "in the head" of the manager. There are five major reasons for committing these plans to paper:

1. Budgeting requires management to examine alternatives before selecting a particular course of action. For example, the quality of the golf course must be considered prior to setting greens fees for the season, especially if there is expected to be a major change in the care and upkeep of the course.

2. Budgeting provides a standard of comparison. At the end of the month, management is able to compare the actual operating results to the budgeted numbers. Significant differences should then be analyzed to suggest the probable cause(s), which require additional investigation and possibly corrective action.

3. Budgeting enables management to look forward, especially when strategic planning is concerned. Too often, managers, including the course superintendent, are either solving current problems or reviewing the past. Budgeting requires management to anticipate the future, especially when considering capital improvement decisions.

4. When participative budgeting is practical, the budget process involves all levels of the course's management. This process motivates lower level managers, because they have real input in the budget process, rather than being forced to adhere to budget numbers that have been imposed upon them by others.

5. The budget process provides a channel of communication whereby the course enterprise's objectives are communicated to the lowest managerial levels. When the budget is used as a standard of comparison, the monthly operating results are also communicated to the various departmental managers, including the golf course superintendent.

In a recent survey, of these five major purposes of budgeting, managers of country clubs have ranked the first two as the most important for using operating budgets.

THE BUDGET PREPARATION PROCESS

Exhibit 7.1 reflects the overall budget preparation process. The preparation of operating budgets begins with establishing the objectives—especially the financial objectives—of the enterprise for the budget period.

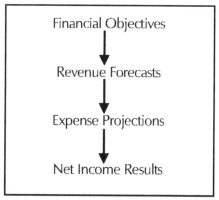

EXHIBIT 7.1. Budget Preparation Process

Objectives

Objectives often include quality of the golf course, number of golf members, and the desired bottom line (net income) results. These objectives are all interrelated and must be clearly communicated by the owner(s) or the board of directors to the executive management team, including the course superintendent.

Since objectives of enterprises change over time, prior to undertaking the revenue forecasts the objectives must be clearly understood by all participants in the budget process.

Forecasting Revenue

Forecasting revenue is the next step in the budgeting process. Revenues vary, depending on the type of golf course enterprise. For a daily fee course with no goods or other services for sale, revenues may be limited to greens fees and golf car rentals. However, at the other extreme, a country club must forecast dues, food sales, beverage sales, and so on. The focus of this chapter will be for the least complex situation, a pay-for-play course with no other goods or services for sale.

In order to forecast revenues, the economic environment, marketing plans, capital improvement budgets, and detailed historical financial results must be considered.

Information regarding the economic environment includes such items as:

◆ Expected inflation for the next (budget) year
◆ Ability of the enterprise to pass cost increases to golfers
◆ Changes in competitive conditions—emergence of new courses, closing of established courses, and so on

In order for this information to be useful, it must be expressed in usable numbers. For example, regarding inflation and the ability of the operation to increase its prices, personnel involved with the budget may be informed that inflation is expected to be 4 percent for the year, and prices for all goods and services will be increased by an average minimum of 4 percent, with 2 percent increases effective January 1 and July 1.

Marketing plans include advertising and promotion plans. For the country club, plans to increase members are part of the marketing effort. For the pay-for-play courses, required information includes the amount of advertising planned for the budget year, how it compares with the past, and what the benefit was from this advertising.

Capital budgeting information includes the timing and cost of expenditures for facilities and equipment. The direct impact on the operations budget is depreciation from a cost perspective. However, other impacts include changing maintenance costs, and in some cases, increased revenues for the golf course.

Historical financial information often serves as the foundation on which course managers build their revenue forecasts. For example, if greens fees have increased by 10 percent each year for the past three years, the enterprise may project a 10 percent increase for the next year. However, other factors, such as advertising expenditures, prices charged, and so on must be carefully considered prior to making this projection.

For illustrative purposes, consider the hypothetical Valley Golf Course. This pay-for-play course's historical revenue information is shown in Exhibit 7.2.

The analysis of the historical information reveals a 10 percent increase in the number of rounds of golf played from 20X5 to 20X6 and also from 20X6 to 20X7. In addition, the analysis shows a 10 percent increase each year in the greens fees.

For purposes of this illustration, it will be assumed that marketing expenses increased by 10 percent for each year and that a further 10 percent increase is planned for the 20X7 budget year.

	20X5	20X6	20X7
Number of rounds	50,000	55,000	60,500
Greens fees per round	$10	$11	$12.10
Total Greens Fees	$500,000	$605,000	$732,050
Analysis		20X5 to 20X6	20X6 to 20X7
Increases over Prior Year:			
1. Rounds of golf		5,000	5,500
Percent increase		10%	10%
2. Greens fees dollar increase		$1	$1.10
Percent increase		10%	10%

EXHIBIT 7.2. Historical Revenue Information for 20X5 –20X7, Valley Golf Course

Therefore, using historical trends, one might cautiously project a 10 percent increase in rounds and greens fees for 20X8.

Certainly other facts from the economic environment (as discussed above) must be considered. However, based on a 10 percent increase for 20X7, the projected greens fees for 20X8 are $885,781, determined as follows:

Average greens fee per round for 20X7	$12.10
percentage increase planned for 20X8	×0.10
Increase in average greens fee	1.21
20X7 average greens fee	12.10
20X8 projected average greens fee	$13.31
Number of rounds of golf during 20X7	60,500
percentage increase planned for 20X8	× 0.10
Increase in rounds	6,050
20X7 rounds played	60,500
20X8 Projected rounds	66,550

Projected Total Greens Fees for 20X8:
$$\$13.31 \times 66{,}550 = \underline{\$885{,}781}$$

Expense Projection

The next step in the budget formulation process is estimating expenses. Since expenses are categorized both in relation to profit centers and by how they react to changes in volume (fixed/variable), the forecasting of expenses is similar to the approach used in forecasting revenues. Prior to estimating expenses, managers must be provided with basic information:

◆ Expected cost increases for supplies, services, etc.

◆ Labor cost increases, including the cost of benefits and payroll taxes

Department heads of a golf course enterprise estimate their variable expenses in relationship to the activity for their departments. For example, the head of the food and beverage department of a country club may use a food cost percentage of 35 percent for estimating the cost of food sales. So by applying the 35 percent to the projected food sales for the year, the budgeted cost of food sales is determined. The golf course superintendent may project monthly variable labor and related payroll costs at $1.00 per round of golf played. In this case, then, the variable payroll cost is projected as $15,000 for the month when 15,000 rounds are forecast.

Each variable expense may be projected in a number of ways. Variable expense may be projected based on a variable cost percentage. The projected percentage is multiplied by sales, as in the cost of food sold example above. Second, variable expense may be projected based on a cost per unit of activity, that is, $X per round of golf played. Third, variable expense may be projected based on cost per unit and estimated time to complete the required tasks. For variable labor, the inputs are hourly wage costs and estimated hours to be worked.

Fixed expenses are projected based on their estimated or contracted amounts. For example, if a course's chief mechanic will be paid $36,000 for the budget year, then $3,000 is the monthly budgeted expense. For another example, consider the cost of fertilizer for the course. The superintendent must project the tonnage and the cost per ton to determine the projected cost expense. Certain fixed expenses are based on "insider" information—that is, information available from management. Examples include the salaries of salaried personnel and depreciation of property and equipment. Other fixed expenses are based, at least partly, on information from "outsiders." Examples include the projected cost per ton of fertilizer from the course's supplier, the cost per kilowatt-hour for electricity supplied by the local utility company, and cost of insurance coverage for the course and/or its equipment by the course's insurance agent.

To illustrate the projection of expenses, consider the hypothetical Valley Golf Course (VGC). Exhibit 7.3 contains the historical expense information for 20X6 and projected changes for 20X7. This presentation is purposely simplified.

The 20X6 amounts are shown for each expense category and the fixed/variable relationship to VGC's revenues is shown. For example, salaries include $300,000 of fixed expense and $60,500 of variable expense. For purposes of simplicity, the relationship between the variable portion of salaries and wages and the course's activity is that the variable portion is $1.00 per round played. The projected change in this expense for 20X7 is an increase "proportional" with rounds. Therefore, the forecasted rounds of 66,550 times $1.00 (cost per round) equals the projected variable wages for 20X7, or $66,550.

An examination of the other variable expenses for the VGC for 20X6 reveals the following:

✦ Payroll taxes and fringe benefits: 30 percent of total salaries and wages
✦ Repairs and maintenance: 10 percent of total revenue
✦ Supplies: $0.20 per round
✦ Income taxes: 25 percent of pretax income

	20X6 Amount	Projected Change	20X7 Projected Amount
Salaries and Wages			
Fixed	$300,000	5% increase	$315,000
Variable	60,500(1)	increase proportionately with rounds	66,550
Payroll Taxes and benefits (variable)	108,150(2)	increase proportionately with total salaries and wages	114,465
Repairs and maintenance			
Fixed	60,000	4% increase	62,400
Variable	7,320(3)	increase proportionately with revenue	8,858
Supplies			
Fixed	50,000	4% increase	52,000
Variable	12,100(4)	increase proportionately with revenue	13,310
Utilities (fixed)	83,950	increase by $10,000	93,950
Interest Expense (fixed)	30,000	decrease by $5,000	25,000
Depreciation (fixed)	30,000	no change	30,000
Insurance (fixed)	15,000	increase by $3,000	18,000
Property Taxes (fixed)	25,000	increase by $3,000	28,000
Income Taxes	5,533(5)	same rate as for 20X6	14,562

(1) $1.00 per round
(2) 30% of total salaries and wages
(3) 1% of revenue
(4) $0.20 per round
(5) 25% of pretax income

EXHIBIT 7.3. Historical Expense Information, Valley Golf Course

Exhibit 7.4 contains the 20X7 operating budget of the Valley Golf Course. The bottom line of $43,686 is based on revenues of $885,781 and total expenses including income taxes of $842,095.

Revenues		$885,781
Expenses		
Salaries and wages	$381,550	
Payroll taxes and benefits	114,465	
Repairs and maintenance	71,258	
Supplies	65,310	
Utilities	93,950	
Interest expense	25,000	
Depreciation	30,000	
Insurance	18,000	
Property taxes	28,000	827,533
Income before Income Taxes		58,248
Income Taxes		14,562
Net Income		$ 43,686

EXHIBIT 7.4. 20X7 Operating Budget, Valley Golf Course

Projected Bottom Line

The projected bottom line of the enterprise is compared to the profit objective. When the objective is satisfied, then the budget is formally presented to the appropriate committees and the Board of Directors or owner of the course. Often operating budgets must be reworked several times before the profit objective is met.

BUDGETARY CONTROL

Operating budgets should be the standard of comparison used by the course's executive team on a periodic basis. Generally, at the end of each month the actual results are compared to budgeted amounts. Major deviations are determined and analyzed, and corrective action should be taken.

The recommended control process consists of five steps:

1. Determine budget variances.
2. Determine significant variances.
3. Analyze significant variances.
4. Determine cause(s) of problems.
5. Take corrective action.

A comparison of the monthly actual numbers against the budget for the month reveals the budget variances. This process is part of the accounting process and is shown on the monthly statement of income and expense. There will most likely be budget variances for most expenses, since the operating budget is simply based on estimates. No budgeting process, however sophisticated, is perfect. Consider the golf course operations schedule for July 20X6 of an actual course, as shown in Exhibit 7.5. (We have used the ABC course as the assigned name for the anonymous but actual course.) This schedule shows the actual and budgeted amounts for July 20X6. The dollar differences are shown and comments are provided for several major differences.

In Step 2 of the control process, significant variances are determined. Only significant variances are analyzed. A variance is considered significant if the amount exceeds a preestablished amount *and* that amount exceeds a preestablished percentage of the budgeted amount. For example, assume the utilities expense is budgeted for $5,000 for the month, and dual criteria for determining variance significance are $400 and 5 percent. Further assume that the actual utilities expense for the month is $5,500. Then the budget variance for utilities expense is $500, which is 10 percent of the budgeted amount. Therefore, the budget variance is significant because it exceeds the preestablished criteria of $400 and 5 percent. The variance in this illustration is *unfavorable* because it is an expense and the actual expense exceeds the budgeted amount. (A revenue item that exceeds the budget would be considered favorable.)

Significant variances are analyzed to determine information useful for detecting the cause(s) of the variance. Finally, the corrective action must be taken.

Both significant revenue and expense variances should be analyzed. However, for purposes of this book, discussion will be limited to variable expenses.

A generic approach to analysis of variable expense variances is to determine the rate and usage variances. This process will be briefly discussed and illustrated.

The basic equations suggested are as follows:

Usage portion: $\qquad\qquad UV = AR(BU - AU)$

where UV = usage variances
$\qquad AR$ = actual rate
$\qquad BU$ = budgeted usage
$\qquad AU$ = actual usage

Account	Actual	Budgeted	Difference	Comment
Contract Labor	$ 2,000	$ 1,000	($1,000)	Landscape service used
Dues and subscriptions	$ 550	$ 450	($ 100)	
Education	$ 800	$ 850	$ 50	
Electric				
Building	$ 1,450	$ 1,300	($ 150)	
Course	$ 475	$ 400	($ 75)	
Pumps	$ 8,800	$ 6,000	($ 2,800)	No rain in July
Equipment rentals	$ 500	$ 0	($ 500)	Rented compressor
Fertilizers and chemicals				
Fertilizers	$ 10,000	$ 10,000	$ 0	
Fungicides	$ 5,000	$ 4,000	($ 1,000)	Brown patch!
Herbicides	$ 1,000	$ 1,000	$ 0	
Insecticides	$ 4,000	$ 2,000	($ 2,000)	Merit (Spring skunks)
Fuels				
Gas	$ 1,800	$ 1,750	($ 50)	
Diesel	$ 2,400	$ 2,200	($ 200)	
Insurance	$ 1,800	$ 1,750	($ 50)	
Motor oils and lubricants	$ 380	$ 375	($ 5)	
Office supplies	$ 150	$ 150	$ 0	
Payroll				
Wages	$ 68,000	$ 58,000	($10,000)	
Insurance	$ 5,200	$ 4,500	($ 700)	
Taxes	$ 6,800	$ 5,800	($ 1,000)	Added employee
Repairs and maintenance				
Equipment	$ 5,400	$ 4,000	($ 1,400)	LF100 needed
Building	$ 1,200	$ 1,500	$ 300	overhaul
Course ground	$ 3,800	$ 4,000	$ 200	
Course fixtures	$ 4,000	$ 4,500	$ 500	
Sand	$ 2,000	$ 2,400	$ 400	Used cheaper sand
Supplies				
Maintenance	$ 880	$ 750	($ 130)	
Course	$ 1,800	$ 2,000	$ 200	
Topdressing	$ 3,890	$ 3,600	($ 290)	Gene increased price
Topsoil	$ 1,200	$ 1,000	($ 200)	
Vehicles	$ 2,200	$ 2,350	$ 150	
Totals	$153,475	$132,425	($21,050)	

EXHIBIT 7.5. Golf Course Operations, ABC Course, July 20X6

Rate portion: $RV = BU(BR - AR)$

where RV = rate variance

BR = budgeted rate

The sum of the usage variance and the rate variance equals the budget variance for the expense item.

To illustrate variance analysis, consider the Valley Golf Course used previously in this chapter. Assume the variable wages budget is $15,000 for June 20X7. This budget was based on $1.00 per round, and for June 20X7, 15,000 rounds were forecast. The average wage paid to employees receiving an hourly wage is $7.50. Therefore, the estimated time to be worked based on the budget is 2,000 hours for the month.

The actual variable labor expense totaled $13,770, which is $1,230 less than the budget. Exhibit 7.6 contains the analysis of the favorable budget variance.

The results include a favorable usage variance of $2,430, which is determined by multiplying the 300 unused hours by the average hourly rate of $8.10. The unfavorable rate variance of $1,200 is determined by multiplying the budgeted hours by the excessive hourly rate of $0.60 per hour.

This analysis directs the superintendent to review the causes of the usage and rate variances. The superintendent should determine the causes of each variance and take corrective action. For example, the $0.60 per hour usage rate difference could be due to overtime pay. Only a thorough investigation will reveal the cause. In addition, the superintendent should investigate

	Hours	Hourly Rate	Total
Budget	2,000	$7.50	$15,000
Actual	1,700	8.10	13,770
		Budget variance	$ 1,230 (F)

$UV = \$8.10\ (2,000 - 1,700)$
$UV = \$8.10\ (300)$
$UV = \underline{\$2,430}\ (F)$

$RV = 2,000\ (\$ 7.50 - \$8.10)$
$RV = 2,000\ (- \$0.60)$
$RV = \underline{1,200}\ (U)$

Budget variance = $UV + RV$
Budget variance = 2,430 (F) – 1,200 (U)
Budget variance = $\underline{\$1,230}$ (F)

EXHIBIT 7.6. Budget Variance Analysis, Valley Golf Course

underutilization of variable labor by 300 hours for the month. Relevant questions include, but are not limited to, the following:

◆ Was maintenance of the course adequate?
◆ Were the rounds of golf played less than projected, leading to this apparent cost savings?

In order for the budgetary control process to be successful, corrective action must be taken when required. The failure to take corrective action may result in future variances that affect both the operation and its bottom line.

COMPUTERIZATION

Budgeting lends itself to computerization. There are several software programs written specifically for golf courses. These programs automatically perform many detailed calculations, freeing the superintendent to more fully consider the major concerns of planning. In addition, the computer may be used to consider alternative scenarios very easily. Since the computer performs the basic mathematical functions, the superintendent has only to input different revenues and costs for each scenario. This process enables the superintendent to determine just what revenues and costs are necessary to achieve the desired bottom-line goals of a golf course operation. However, regardless of the level of computerization, the budget for course maintenance is still the responsibility of the superintendent, and the output (budget results) is no better than the inputs!

SUMMARY

Operating budgets reflect projected revenues and expenses of the golf course enterprise. The steps in the budget preparation process are (1) establish objectives, (2) forecast revenues, (3) project expenses, and (4) determine the net income results. Many superintendents focus their budgeting efforts on expenses, since they are not responsible for course revenues. Projected expenses, including both fixed and variable expenses, must be carefully projected, based on historical information and expected future changes.

The budgetary control process consists of five steps: (1) determining budget variances, (2) determining which variances are significant, (3) analyzing significant variances (4) determining the cause(s) of significant variances, and (5) taking corrective action. Failure to take the required corrective action may render the control process useless.

PROBLEMS

Problem 1

The manager of the Mountain Top Golf Course (MTGC) wants your assistance in forecasting its revenues and labor costs for 20X7. This course's activities are limited to golf and a snack bar; however, the snack bar is operated by an independent contractor who pays the MTGC $10,000 of rental income annually. Information for 20X5 and 20X6 and expected changes for 20X7 are as follows:

	20X5	20X6	Expected changes for 20X7
Rounds of golf	40,000	42,000	Increase by 5%
Greens fees	$ 11	$ 12	$13—increase by $1.00
Rental income	$ 10,000	$ 10,000	No change
Salaries and wages			
Fixed	$200,000	$220,000	Increase by 8%
Variable	$ 40,000	$ 42,000	Increase by $0.10 per round
Benefits and payroll taxes:	$ 36,000	$ 39,300	Increase to 16% of total salaries and wages

Required:
1. Forecast the revenue for 20X7.
2. Project the labor costs for 20X7.

Problem 2

Golfers played 6,000 rounds at the MTGC during June 20X6. The variable wages expense was budgeted at $6,000 based on 1,000 hours at $6.00 per hour. The actual wage expense totaled $6,820 based on 1,100 hours of work.

Required:
1. Determine the budget variance for the wages expense for June 20X6.
2. Conduct variance analysis as follows:
   a. Determine the usage variance.
   b. Determine the rate variance.
3. Suggest possible causes of the variances determined in Part 2.

MULTIPLE CHOICE QUESTIONS

1. The focus of the _____ budget is revenues and expenses.
   a. cash
   b. capital improvements
   c. operations
   d. all of the above

2. The best standard for comparing the operating results for this month is
   a. the competition.
   b. last month's operating results.
   c. the same month's operating results for the prior year.
   d. the operating budget.

3. The initial step in the budget process is
   a. establishing financial objectives.
   b. forecasting revenue.
   c. projecting expenses.
   d. projecting net income.

4. The ABC Club projects its green fees based on its average greens fee and the trend of rounds played. The number of rounds played during June of 20X4 to 20X6 has been 10,000, 11,000, and 12,000, respectively. The green fee per round for 20X7 has been set at $15.00. The projected greens fees for June 20X7 are _____.
   a. $165,000
   b. $180,000
   c. $195,000
   d. none of the above

5. The budgetary control process is completed when
   a. budget variances are determined.
   b. significant budget variances are identified.
   c. budget variances are analyzed.
   d. management takes corrective action.

8

Capital Budgeting

In the discussion of operating budgets in the prior chapter, a distinction was made between operating and capital budgets. The superintendent's operating budget includes the day-by-day expenses of maintaining the golf course. The benefits from operating expenses are expected to last less than one operating period. In contrast, capital expenditures are defined as cash outflows for property and equipment.

The coverage of capital budgeting in this chapter will provide answers to the following questions: How can capital expenditures be cost justified? How are future project cash flows discounted? What is meant by net present value? What is the time value of money? What is the payback approach to capital budgeting?

The superintendent will determine that one or more capital expenditure projects would benefit the course. These projects will then be proposed to the board, typically as a part of the budgeting process. Generally the superintendent and the board will have more capital proposals than they will have cash to fund them; thus, some method(s) are required for choosing the most appropriate ones.

Basically, then, we are discussing ranking and selecting capital investment proposals. If the proposal is accepted, the cost of the proposal will be shown on the Balance Sheet (as a new asset) after the expenditures have been made, and the impact of having the investment will show up on the Income Statement as an increase in revenue, with a corresponding increase in expenses (for capital projects resulting in revenues), or possibly simply an overall decrease in expenses as compared to expected results if the capital expenditure were not made.

This chapter begins with the descriptions of some capital investment projects and continues with the identification of cash flows related to these projects. Also covered in this chapter are the concepts of the time value of money and two capital budgeting evaluation models—namely, payback and net present value.

CAPITAL INVESTMENT DECISIONS

Some typical capital investment decisions face the golfing enterprise from time to time:

- ✦ *Replace or repair/keep?* As equipment or facilities become nearly "used up" the decision must be made about whether to repair them and use them longer or replace them with new items. Generally, the older these items are, the more costly the ongoing maintenance.
- ✦ *Purchase capital item A or B?* When buying a new machine, the enterprise usually has a choice among different brands, sizes, performance characteristics, and so on. Although much of the decision can be based on technical differences, a major consideration has to be the economic differences between competing proposals.
- ✦ *Lease or buy?* Golf courses often have the option to either buy equipment or lease it. Differences in the economics of the two options should be considered. This will be discussed in some detail in Chapter 9.
- ✦ *Do it yourself or hire it out?* Much maintenance work can either be done by golf course personnel or by outside contractors. Economic differences often can be the deciding factor.

These capital investment decisions occur occasionally throughout the year, rather than as daily operating decisions. Ideally, superintendents anticipate these major changes and carefully plan for them.

ESTIMATING THE FLOW OF FUNDS

The process of evaluating capital investments should generally be based on a comparison of forecasted cash inflows and cash outflows related to each project. In general, the projects with the largest excess inflows over outflows are the ones selected to be included in the capital budget. If outflows are estimated to be greater than inflows, the investment will result in a loss, and should be rejected, except in rare situations. When more than one investment project has positive net cash inflows, and the enterprise wants to limit the number of projects to be undertaken, then those with the largest excess of inflows over outflows are the most economically desirable.

Cash inflows and outflows must be forecast as accurately as possible. These two streams of funds must be compared in order to decide which option is most economically desirable.

1. **Inflows.** The proposed investment project is expected to generate a flow of cash for the business. The funds may come from additional revenues, as in the case of a proposed investment in a snack bar or golf car rental operation. Or, more commonly for the course maintenance, the proposed investment will generate a cost saving over the present operation, as when installing an automated irrigation system to reduce labor costs.

    It is important to consider all net cash inflows involved with the proposed investment, including estimated salvage value of the item.

2. **Outflows**. A major outflow of funds will be the initial cost of the proposed capital investment. Essentially, this is what will be compared to the net inflows to determine the economic feasibility of the proposed investment. Other outflows during the life of the investment might include planned overhauls of a proposed piece of equipment, as well as installation costs, training costs, and costs of operations.

    Thus, from a timing perspective, cash outflows occur when the investment is made—that is, the cash outflow is equal to the cost of the investment, while the net inflows or cost savings occur throughout the useful life of the item. Assume five golf cars are purchased at the cost of $4,000 apiece. Then the total cash outflow now is $20,000. As the cars are rented to members, cash inflow occurs. The cash inflow occurs throughout the life of the cars. However, operating expenses related to the use of the cars also occur throughout the life of the cars. Since the cash inflows and outflows occur in part at different times, they must be placed on an "equal" basis in order to compare them. This process will be discussed in more detail later in this chapter.

TECHNIQUES FOR EVALUATING
CAPITAL INVESTMENT PROPOSALS

Depending on the characteristics of capital investment proposals, various analysis techniques can be applied to evaluate them. One such technique—the payback approach—is easy to apply, but is less precise in evaluating forecast investment cash flows. It is effective in making preliminary screenings of proposals and for roughly comparing competing proposals, but ideally it should be used only when the following situations exist:

1. The proposal covers a relatively short time period (three to five years).
2. The patterns of funds flow in competing proposals are relatively comparable in their timing.

A superior capital budgeting evaluation model is the net present value approach. This approach considers not only the cash flows related to the proposed investment project, but also the timing of the cash flows. Both the payback and net present value approaches will be presented and illustrated in this chapter. However, the concept of the time value of money will be discussed first.

Time Value of Money

The saying, "$100 today is worth more than $100 a year from now," is true—in part because $100 today could be invested to provide $100 plus the interest for one year into the future. If the $100 can be invested at 10 percent annual interest, then the $100 will be worth $110 in one year. This is determined as follows:

Principal + (Principal × Time × Interest Rate) = Total
$100 + ($100 × 1 × 0.10) = $110

Principal is the sum of dollars at the beginning of the investment period ($100 in this case). *Time* is expressed in years, as long as an annual interest rate is used. The interest rate is expressed in decimal form. The interest earned of $10 for the year plus the principal of $100 equals the amount available one year hence.

A shorter formula for calculating a future value is as follows:

$$F = A(1 + I)^n$$

where F = future value
A = present amount
I = interest rate
n = number of years (or interest periods)

One hundred dollars invested at 10 percent for two years will yield $121.00, determined as follows:

$$F = 100 (1 + 0.10)^2$$
$$F = 100 (1.21)$$
$$F = \underline{\$121.00}$$

The concept of present value must be introduced, since it is used extensively with the net present value capital budgeting model to be discussed later in this chapter. For future values, one determines the value a present sum will grow to at a future date. The present value concept asks, "What is the value today of future amount?" In essence, present value is the reverse of future value.

The present value of a future amount is the amount today that must be invested at some interest rate (x%) to yield the future amount. For example what is the present value of $110 one year hence when the annual interest rate is 10 percent? From our previous calculations we know it is $100. So what is the present value of $100 one year hence, given an interest rate of 10 percent?

The formula to determine the present value of the future amount is as follows:

$$P = F \frac{1}{(1+I)^n}$$

where P = present amount
F = future amount
I = interest rate
n = number of years

Therefore, the present value of $100 one year hence (assume an interest rate of 10%) is $90.91, determined as follows:

$$P = 100 \frac{1}{(1+0.10)^1}$$
$$P = 100(0.9091)$$
$$P = \$90.91$$

The present value of $100 two years hence (assuming an interest rate of 10%) is $82.64, determined as follows:

$$P = 100 (0.8264)$$
$$P = \underline{\$82.64}$$

An alternative to using this formula to calculate the present value of a future amount is to use a table of present value factors, such as that found in Exhibit 8.1. The present value factors in Exhibit 8.1 are based on future amounts at the end of the period. For example, the present value of $100 a year from now at 15 percent interest is $86.96. This is determined by finding the number in the 15 percent column and the period 1 row (0.8696) and multiplying it by $100. The present value of $100 today is simply $100.

The present value of a future amount will vary significantly based on the interest rate and the timing of the future cash flows. Everything else being the same, the higher the discount rate, the lower the present value. Likewise, everything else being the same, the more distant the receipt, the smaller the present value.

Many capital investments provide a stream of cash inflows for several years. When the amounts are equal and are at equal time intervals, such as the end of each year, the stream is referred to as an annuity. Exhibit 8.2 shows the calculation of the present value of an annuity (at 15%) of $10,000 due at the end of each year for five years. The present value factors used in the calculation are from the present value table in Exhibit 8.1.

An alternative to multiplying each future amount by a separate present value factor from the present value table in Exhibit 8.1 is to sum the present factors to make one multiplication. This is illustrated in Exhibit 8.3. Thus, the $33,522 calculated in Exhibit 8.3 equals the calculations performed in Exhibit 8.2. Rather than using the present values from Exhibit 8.1, present values for an annuity are provided in Exhibit 8.4. As a check on your understanding of the present value of an annuity table, locate the present value factor for five years and 15 percent. As you would expect, it is 3.3522. Thus, the present value for an annuity is nothing more than a summation of present value factors from Exhibit 8.1. However, this table of present value factors for an annuity will save much time, especially when the present value of streams of receipts for several years must be calculated.

Two Common Techniques for Evaluating Capital Investment Proposals

Some capital investment evaluation techniques—such as calculating the payback period—are easy to apply but are less precise in evaluating proposed investments.

Since the payback approach is commonly used by top management for making quick decisions, it is important to know how it is used and to know its shortcomings.

Number of Periods	1%	2%	3%	4%	5%	6%	7%	8%	9%	10%	12%	14%	15%
1	0.9901	0.9804	0.9709	0.9615	0.9524	0.9434	0.9346	0.9259	0.9174	0.9091	0.8929	0.8772	0.8696
2	0.9803	0.9612	0.9426	0.9246	0.9070	0.8900	0.8734	0.8573	0.8417	0.8264	0.7972	0.7695	0.7561
3	0.9706	0.9423	0.9151	0.8890	0.8638	0.8396	0.8163	0.7938	0.7722	0.7513	0.7118	0.6750	0.6575
4	0.9610	0.9238	0.8885	0.8548	0.8227	0.7921	0.7629	0.7350	0.7084	0.6830	0.6355	0.5921	0.5718
5	0.9515	0.9057	0.8626	0.8219	0.7835	0.7473	0.7130	0.6806	0.6499	0.6209	0.5674	0.5194	0.4972
6	0.9420	0.8880	0.8375	0.7903	0.7462	0.7050	0.6663	0.6302	0.5963	0.5645	0.5066	0.4556	0.4323
7	0.9327	0.8706	0.8131	0.7599	0.7107	0.6651	0.6227	0.5835	0.5470	0.5132	0.4523	0.3996	0.3759
8	0.9235	0.8535	0.7894	0.7307	0.6768	0.6274	0.5820	0.5403	0.5019	0.4665	0.4039	0.3506	0.3269
9	0.9143	0.8368	0.7664	0.7026	0.6446	0.5919	0.5439	0.5002	0.4604	0.4241	0.3606	0.3075	0.2843
10	0.9053	0.8203	0.7441	0.6756	0.6139	0.5584	0.5083	0.4632	0.4224	0.3855	0.3220	0.2697	0.2472
11	0.8963	0.8043	0.7224	0.6496	0.5847	0.5268	0.4751	0.4289	0.3875	0.3505	0.2875	0.2366	0.2149
12	0.8874	0.7885	0.7014	0.6246	0.5568	0.4970	0.4440	0.3971	0.3555	0.3186	0.2567	0.2076	0.1869
13	0.8787	0.7730	0.6810	0.6006	0.5303	0.4688	0.4150	0.3677	0.3262	0.2897	0.2292	0.1821	0.1625
14	0.8700	0.7579	0.6611	0.5775	0.5051	0.4423	0.3878	0.3405	0.2992	0.2633	0.2046	0.1597	0.1413
15	0.8613	0.7430	0.6419	0.5553	0.4810	0.4173	0.3624	0.3152	0.2745	0.2394	0.1827	0.1401	0.1229
16	0.85280	0.7284	0.6232	0.5399	0.4581	0.3936	0.3387	0.2919	0.2519	0.2176	0.1631	0.1229	0.1069
17	0.84440	0.7142	0.6050	0.5134	0.4363	0.3714	0.3166	0.2703	0.2311	0.1978	0.1456	0.1078	0.0929
18	0.83600	0.7002	0.5874	0.4936	0.4155	0.3503	0.2959	0.2502	0.2120	0.1799	0.1300	0.0946	0.0808
19	0.82770	0.6864	0.5703	0.4746	0.3957	0.3305	0.2765	0.2317	0.1945	0.1635	0.1161	0.0826	0.0703
20	0.81950	0.6730	0.5530	0.4564	0.3769	0.3118	0.2584	0.2145	0.1784	0.1486	0.1037	0.0728	0.0611

EXHIBIT 8.1. Abbreviated Table of Present Value Factor for a Single Cash Flow

131

Present Value	Years in Future				
	1	2	3	4	5
Amount	$10,000	$10,000	$10,000	$10,000	$10,000
$ 8,696	0.8696				
7,561		0.7561			
6,575			0.6575		
5,718				0.5718	
4,972					0.4972
Total $33,522					

EXHIBIT 8.2. Present Value of a $10,000 Five-Year Annuity at 15%

Years Hence	Present Value Factor at 15%
1	0.8696
2	0.7561
3	0.6575
4	0.5718
5	+ 0.4972
	3.3522

3.3522 × $10,000 = $33,522

EXHIBIT 8.3. Shortcut Calculations of the Present Value of a $10,000 Five-Year Annuity at 15%

More refined analysis approaches yield more precise evaluation. These approaches include calculating the net present value of an investment's cash flows. This technique is preferred if the investments are relatively large, if the period of inflows/outflows is long, or if there are substantial differences in the timing of the flows.

The remainder of the chapter is devoted to explaining these two capital investment analysis tools. It is important to determine the time periods over which the related cash flows will occur, not just the average amount of the flows. In all of the examples that follow, the earnings or savings are net of all future operating costs associated with the proposed expenditure. For example, if a proposed project will yield annual cash inflow of $10,000 but require $5,000 of cash outflow annually, the net cash inflow will be $5,000.

DETERMINING THE PAYBACK PERIOD

As its name implies, the payback period is the number of years it will take for a project to generate net inflows of cash equal to the cost of the project, thereby paying for itself out of its own earnings. Generally, the shorter the payback period, the better the investment. Of course, the payback period must be shorter than the expected life of the proposed capital investment project.

Suppose proposed machines that cost $20,000 can save the enterprise $5,000 in each of its five useful years. How many years will it take to recover its cost? The answer is found below:

Cash outflow	=	$20,000
Cash savings	=	

Year		Amount
1		$ 5,000
2		$ 5,000
3		$ 5,000
4		$ 5,000
5		$ 5,000
	Total	$25,000

After five years, $25,000 will be recovered in the form of labor savings. To reach $20,000 in cost savings, four years is required. So the payback period is four years.

In general, the payback period is determined by the following equation:

$$\text{Payback period} = \frac{\text{Cost of investment}}{\text{Annual net cash inflow or savings}}$$

To use the payback approach for comparing two or more proposals, calculate the payback period for each. Then select the one with the shortest period and reject any whose payback period is longer than (a) the useful life of the asset, or (b) the investment guidelines provided by upper management.

The following example shows how to evaluate several projects using payback as the selection criterion. A superintendent has developed four invest-

Number of Periods	1%	2%	3%	4%	5%	6%	7%	8%	9%	10%	12%	14%	15%
1	0.9901	0.9804	0.9709	0.9615	0.9524	0.9434	0.9346	0.9259	0.9174	0.9091	0.8929	0,8772	0.8696
2	1.9704	1.9416	1.9135	1.8861	1.8594	1.8334	1.8080	1.7833	1.7591	1.7355	1.6901	1,6467	1.6257
3	2.9410	2.8839	2.8286	2.7751	2.7232	2.6730	2.6243	2.5771	2.5313	2.4869	2.4018	2.3216	2.2832
4	3.9020	3.8077	3.7171	3.6299	3.5460	3.4651	3.3872	3.3121	3.2397	3.1699	3.0373	2.9137	2.8550
5	4.8534	4.7135	4.5797	4.4518	4.3295	4.2124	4.1002	3.9927	3.8897	3.7908	3.6048	3.4331	3.3522
6	5.7955	5.6014	5,4172	5.2421	5.0757	4.9173	4.7665	4.6229	4.4859	4.3553	4.1114	3.8887	3.7845
7	6.7282	6.4720	6.2303	6.0021	5.7864	5.5824	5.3893	5.2064	5.0330	4.8684	4.5638	4.2883	4.1604
8	7.6517	7.3255	7.0197	6.7327	6.4632	6.2098	5.9713	5.7466	5.5348	5.3349	4.9676	4.6389	4.4873
9	8.5660	8.1622	7.7861	7.4353	7.1078	6.8017	6.5152	6.2469	5.9952	5.7590	5.3282	4.9464	4.7716
10	9.4713	8.8926	8.5302	8.1109	7.7217	7.3601	7.0236	6.7101	6.4177	6.1446	5.6502	5.2161	5.0188
11	10.3676	9.7868	9.2526	8.7605	8.3064	7.8869	7.4987	7.1390	6.8052	6.4951	5.9377	5.4527	5.2337
12	11.2551	10.5753	9.9540	9.3851	8.8633	8.3838	7.9427	7.5361	7.1607	6.8137	6.1944	5.6603	5.4206
13	12.1337	11.3484	10.6350	9.9856	9.3936	8.8527	8.3577	7.9038	7.4869	7.1034	6.4235	5.8424	5.5831
14	13.0037	12.1062	11.2961	10.5631	9.8986	9.2950	8.7455	8.2442	7.7862	7.3667	6.6282	6.0021	5.7245
15	13.8651	12.8493	11.9379	11.1184	10.3797	9.7122	9.1079	8.5595	8.0607	7.6061	6.8109	6.1422	5.8474
16	14.7179	13.5777	12.5611	11.6523	10.8378	10.1059	9.4466	8.8514	8.3126	7.8237	6.9740	6.2651	5.9542
17	15.5623	14.2919	13.1661	12.1657	11.2741	10.4773	9.7632	9.1216	8.5436	8.0216	7.1196	6.3729	6.0472
18	16.3983	14.9220	13.7535	12.6593	11.6896	10.8276	10.0591	9.3719	8.7556	8.2014	7.2497	6.4674	6.1280
19	17.2260	15.6785	14.3238	13.1339	12.0853	11.1581	10.3356	9.6036	8.9501	8.3649	7.3658	6.5504	6.1982
20	18.0456	16.3514	14.8775	13.5903	12.4622	11.4699	10.5940	9,8181	9.1285	8.5136	7.4694	6.6231	6.2593

EXHIBIT 8.4. Abbreviated Table of Present Value Factors for an Annuity

ment proposals, each oriented to provide cost savings. The cash inflows and outflows for each are as follows:

Year	Proposal A Cost	Proposal A Cash Savings	Proposal B Cost	Proposal B Cash Savings	Proposal C Cost	Proposal C Cash Savings	Proposal D Cost	Proposal D Cash Savings
1	$15,000	$5,000	$15,000	$3,000	$15,000	$2,000	$15,000	$4,000
2		5,000		3,000		2,000		4,000
3		5,000		3,000		2,000		4,000
4		5,000		3,000		2,000		4,000
5		0		3,000		2,000		4,000
6		0		3,000		2,000		4,000
7		0		0		0		4,000
Average annual cash savings		$5,000		$3,000		$2,000		$4,000
Payback period		3 years		5 years		Not achieved		3.75 years
Useful life		4 years		6 years		6 years		7 years

The payback period can be of some use in screening the four proposals. Proposal A seems to be better than Proposal B—the shorter payback period is clearly better. Proposal C can be excluded outright—its initial cost exceeds future cash savings, so it does not pay for itself. Proposal D has a longer life than Proposal A and provides a greater amount of cash savings; however, its payback period is longer. Therefore, with payback, Proposal A is accepted.

This method has several shortcomings that limit its usefulness. First, the method does not consider the earnings that continue after the payback period is reached. Proposal D, for instance, has a total savings of $28,000, in comparison to the $20,000 total earnings of Proposal A. The slightly shorter payback of Proposal A may mislead the superintendent who relies solely on the payback approach to evaluating investments. Also, keep in mind that we are ignoring the time value of money of the cash savings for each proposal when using the payback approach.

These shortcomings are overcome by using the more sophisticated net present value approach.

CALCULATING THE NET PRESENT VALUE

The net present value of an investment proposal is determined by comparing the present value of all cash inflows with the cost of the investment proposal. The investment proposal must have a positive net present value to be attractive; that is, the present value of the cash inflows must be equal to or larger than the cost of the investment. When comparing two alternatives, the one with the larger net present value would be selected, providing the enterprise has the funds needed for the investment.

Future cash flows are discounted using the interest rate the enterprise would have to pay if funds were borrowed to finance the proposed investment. For example, if the enterprise would have to borrow funds at a 12 percent annual interest rate, then 12 percent should be used in the net present value approach. Alternatively, if an investment will be liquidated to pay for the proposed investment rather than borrowing funds, the rate of return on this investment could be used as the discount rate. If there is doubt regarding the proper rate, the course superintendent should consider asking the chief financial executive of the golfing enterprise for assistance with the appropriate rate.

Proposals A and D from the example presented earlier are used to illustrate the net present value approach, as follows:

Year	Proposal A Initial Cost	Proposal A Cash Savings	Proposal D Initial Cost	Proposal D Cash Savings
1	$15,000	$5,000	$15,000	$4,000
2		5,000		4,000
3		5,000		4,000
4		5,000		4,000
5		0		4,000
6		0		4,000
7		0		4,000

The net present value of Proposal A is (using a 10% annual interest rate) as follows:

Earnings	×	PV Factor	=	Present Value
$ 5,000	×	0.9091	=	$ 4,546
5,000	×	0.8264	=	4,132
5,000	×	0.7513	=	3,757
5,000	×	0.6830	=	3,415
		Present value	=	15,850
		Initial investment	=	<15,000>
		Net present value	=	$ 850

Proposal A has a net present value of $850.00.

This proposal is earning just over the required 10 percent return. Even though cash savings total $20,000 over its useful life, when considering the time value of money, the excess is less than $1,000.

The net present value of Proposal D is (using a 10% annual interest rate) as follows:

Earnings	×	PV factor	=	Present value
$4,000	×	0.9091	=	$ 3,636
$4,000	×	0.8264	=	3,306
$4,000	×	0.7513	=	3,005
$4,000	×	0.6830	=	2,732
$4,000	×	0.6209	=	2,484
$4,000	×	0.5645	=	2,258
$4,000	×	0.5132	=	2,053
		Present value	=	19,474
		Initial investment	=	<15,000>
		Net present value	=	$ 4,474

Proposal D has net present value that is greater than the initial investment cost-it is earning something more than the required 10 percent return. Proposal D has the higher net present value, due to the fact that the earnings are received over a longer period of time. This analysis indicates that Proposal D should be selected over Proposal A. Remember that the payback approach suggested that Proposal A would be selected over D, since its payback period was shorter. This illustration clearly indicates the superiority of the net present value approach over the payback approach for selecting mutually exclusive capital investment projects.

SUMMARY

Capital budgeting focuses on the acquisition of facilities and equipment. The two methods presented for determining acceptable projects are payback and net present value. Both of these approaches consider the cash flows related to the proposed project. First, there is the initial cash outflow, which is the cost of the investment. Second, there may be cash inflows and cash outflows or cash savings over the life of the investment.

The payback approach determines the number of years required for a project to pay for itself. This approach is best used for screening projects for further consideration using the net present value approach.

The net present value approach considers both the amount of the cash flows and the timing of the cash flows. Using present value factors, future cash flows are discounted to the present time and compared to the initial cost of the project. When considering a single proposal, if the net present value of a proposed investment is equal to zero or is positive, the investment should be made.

PROBLEMS

Problem 1

The Golden Ridge Golf Course has decided to erect a fence to keep intruders off its golf course. The estimated cost of the fence is $20,000, and annual maintenance is expected to be $2,000. The fence is expected to have a useful life of 20 years. The value of the benefits is expected to be as follows:

- Eliminate vandalism to the course, which is costing an estimated $4,000 annually.
- Increased play. It is estimated that several partial rounds are played by golfers playing on the back nine without paying. The estimated annual benefit—net of any increased costs—related to more rounds of golf is $2,000.

Required:
Determine the payback period of this capital investment.

Problem 2

The Grissom Golf Club (GGC) has decided to construct forward tees on its 18-hole course. The estimated construction cost is $50,000. The GGC's owner, Gayle Grissom, believes many more rounds of golf will be played and other profit centers will also benefit. Her estimates on an annual basis for ten years are as follows:

a. Increased maintenance = $5,000
b. Increased green fees (2,000 rounds at $10 per round) = $20,000
c. Increased food sales (net of related costs) = $2,000
d. Increased miscellaneous sales (shirts, clubs, etc.) = $8,000
e. Increased cost of miscellaneous sales and related variable costs = $6,000

Required:
1. What are the annual net cash flows?
2. Determine the net present value of this proposed investment given a discount rate of 12 percent.

MULTIPLE CHOICE QUESTIONS

1. The_____ budgets focus on the acquisition of equipment.
   a. operating
   b. capital
   c. cash
   d. all of the above

2. The future value of $100 in three years is___ given   annual compounding and an annual interest rate of 10 percent.
   a. $110
   b. $121
   c. $133.10
   d. $146.41
   e. none of the above

3. The present value of $1,000 a year hence, given a 10 percent interest rate, is _____.
   a. $900
   b. $909.09
   c. $915.21
   d. none of the above

4. The payback approach to capital budgeting ignores
   a. the timing of the cash flows.
   b. cash outflows.
   c. cash inflows.
   d. the cost of the project.

5. The net present value approach considers all but one of the following. Which is not considered?
   a. cost of capital projects
   b. profit from the capital project
   c. cash inflows from the capital project
   d. cash outflows related to the capital project

9

Leasing

An alternative to purchasing equipment is to lease. Leasing is a preferred approach to obtaining equipment when the costs of leasing are less than owning. Several questions related to leasing that superintendents have include the following:

1. Who are the parties to a lease?
2. What are major advantages and disadvantages of leasing?
3. What is the difference between an operating and a capital lease?
4. How do operating and capital leases affect the operation's Income Statement?
5. What factors are relevant in considering a lease or a purchase?

The answers to these questions and others regarding leasing are provided in this chapter.

LEASES AND THEIR USES

A lease is simply an agreement conveying the right to use resources for specified purposes and a limited time. From an operational perspective, the resource is available for use; often operating personnel generally have little concern as to whether the equipment is leased or purchased. However, from a financial perspective, leasing is preferred when it results in lower costs than other options. Lease agreements govern the parties to the lease and vary in length often by the term of the lease. The two parties to a lease are the lessor and the lessee. The lessor owns the equipment and conveys the right of its use to the lessee in exchange for rental payments.

Leasing has been popular in U.S. hospitality businesses, and golf courses in particular. Golf course operations have leased golf cars, mowing equipment, maintenance vehicles, and aeration equipment.

CLASSIFICATION OF LEASES

In general, leases are classified for accounting purposes as either operating leases or capital leases (also known as conditional sales contracts). These two types of leases can differ substantially, although they can also be hard to distinguish at times. Operating leases are normally of relatively short duration, and the lessor retains the responsibility for property taxes (if any), insurance, and maintenance. Often the operating lease will have lower monthly payments than capital leases because the "residual" value at the end of the lease remains with the lessor. The lessee often has the opportunity to purchase the leased item at its fair market value at the end of the lease period. This type of lease is generally easily canceled. If the golf course leased a trencher for one week to install some drainage tile, this lease would certainly be accounted for as an operating lease.

On the other hand, capital leases are of relatively long duration, and the lessee often assumes the responsibility for property taxes (if any), insurance, and maintenance. In addition, these leases are often either noncancelable or fairly costly to cancel. Often the lessee has an option to purchase the leased equipment (under a capital lease) for a nominal amount.

Operating leases and capital leases are accounted for differently. Operating leases are expensed as lease payments are made. For example, assume the cost to rent a trencher for one week is $700. The $700 is recorded as equipment rental expense, and it is reflected on the golf course's operations schedule.

A capital lease is accounted for as if the equipment were purchased. An asset is shown on the firm's balance sheet, as well as a corresponding liability recognizing the golfing enterprise's responsibility to make lease payments in the future to the lessor.

For example, assume a fairway mower is leased for six years. Further, assume that the lease agreement requires $1,000 down and 20 future quarterly payments of $1,500 each. Assume a relevant quarterly interest rate of 3%. The present value of these payments is determined as follows:

Present value of down payment	$ 1,000
Future payments:	
$1,500 × 14.8775[1]	22,316
Total	$23,316

Therefore, this lease is recorded as follows:

Leased equipment	$23,316	
Obligations for lease payments		$22,316
Cash		1,000

This entry recognizes the "cost" of the mower as an asset, the down payment and the present value of future lease payments as a liability.

The enterprise will show the leased equipment on the balance sheet in the asset section as property and equipment and the obligation for lease payments also on the balance sheet as a liability. Expense will be recognized over the time the mower is used as a depreciation expense. In addition, as lease payments are made a portion of each payment is accounted for as interest expense.

Thus, the accounting treatment differs fairly drastically between these two types of leases. With the operating lease, only expense is recognized with each payment. Accounting for the capital lease results in recognition on the balance sheet, and depreciation and interest expenses over time are shown on the income statement.

ADVANTAGES AND DISADVANTAGES OF LEASING

There are several advantages and disadvantages of leasing. The advantages of leasing include the following:

✦ Leasing conserves working capital, because little or no cash is generally deposited to lease property, while cash equal to 20 to 40percent of

---

[1] Value based on 20 periods at 3 percent, from Exhibit 8.4.

the purchase price is required when purchasing property. For the cash-strapped golf course operation, leasing may be the only reasonable way of obtaining the desired equipment. Even when it may be more expensive to lease, due to lack of cash necessary to purchase and/or the inability to qualify for financing, leasing rather than purchasing is used.

✦ Leasing is often less complex than acquiring the property through external financing. Although a lease agreement must be prepared, it usually is less involved than the numerous documents required in a purchase when financing is used.

✦ Leasing permits quicker changes in equipment, especially when equipment becomes functionally obsolete due to technological innovations. (Of course, the lessee cannot expect this ability to be cost-free. The greater the probability of technological obsolescence, the greater the lease payment, all other things being the same.)

✦ Leasing has less negative impact on financial ratios when the leases are not capitalized. Operating leases are not shown on the balance sheet, nor are the future lease obligations.

✦ Leasing is desirable for many golf courses, as they can update to newer equipment at closer intervals (golf cars every 3 to 5 years, mowers every 5 to 7 years).

The disadvantages of leasing include the following:

✦ Any residual value of the leased property benefits the lessor, unless the lessee has the opportunity to acquire the leased property at the end of the lease.

✦ The cost of leasing in some situations is higher than purchasing. This may be especially true when there are only a limited number of lessors and the economic situation is not competitive. An operation may be saddled with extended payments for equipment that becomes dysfunctional or obsolete.

✦ Termination of a capital lease before the end of the lease period often results in additional costs that are not present if the property is owned.

Although this discussion of the advantages and disadvantages of leasing is not exhaustive, it does present the key points to consider when you attempt to decide whether to lease or buy. Let's now look more closely at how to make this decision.

CHOOSING TO LEASE OR BUY

Should a golf course lease or buy property? The elements to consider when answering this question include the effect of the decision on taxes (for courses subject to income taxes) and the time value of money. Each will be considered as we explore the concept of leasing versus buying.

Suppose the management of the hypothetical Valley View Golf Club (VVGC) must decide whether to buy or lease a fairway mower. To begin with, let's consider only the purchase cost of the fairway mower and the lease payments the VVGC would have to make for the buy and lease options. Assume that the purchase cost of the mower is $25,000, while the annual lease payments would be $6,000 at the signing of the lease for the first year and $5,565 for the next four years (paid at the end of years 1 to 4). Further assume that the VVGC is responsible for maintenance with either option. The lease payments total $28,260; therefore, the apparent advantage to the VVGC of buying over leasing is $3,260.

However, we must not forget to consider the time value of money. Assume that the VVGC's relevant interest rate for this scenario is 10%. In order compare the costs of buying and leasing, the present value of the cash payments for each must be determined. The cost of the mower is not discounted, since we assume the mower is paid for with cash at the beginning of the first year. The initial lease payment made at the signing of the lease is not discounted. However, the future lease payments must be discounted to recognize the present value of those payments. Cash flows covering the lease payments for the five-year period should be discounted as follows:

Present value of first payment: $ 6,000

Present value of next four (annuity) payments:

$5,565 $(\text{PVA}_{n=4,k=10})$ = $5,565(3.1699*)   17,640

Total $23,640

This result suggests that leasing the mower would cost $1,360 less ($25,000 – $23,640) than buying it.

However, there are yet other considerations—in particular, taxes and the salvage value of the mower at the end of the five years. Tax considerations for the purchase option involve depreciation expense each year; those for the lease option involve treating the lease payment as an expense each year. Sal-

*From Exhibit 8.4.

vage value must be considered, because under the buy alternative the salvage value provides cash.

Assume that, based on discussions with the equipment dealer, the VVGC's superintendent estimates that the salvage value of the mower will be $6,000—that is, the mower can be sold for $6,000 at the end of year 5. Further assume that the VVGC's tax rate is 30 percent, and that the enterprise

			Time, Years			
	0	**1**	**2**	**3**	**4**	**5**
PURCHASE OPTION						
Purchase price	$25,000					
Salvage value						–6,000
Depreciation tax shield [1]	0	–1,140	–1,140	–1,140	–1,140	–1,140
Net purchase cost						
Annual cash flows	25,000	–1,140	–1,140	–1,140	–1,140	–7,140
Discount factors [2]	×1	×.9091	×.8264	×.7513	×.6830	×.6209
Present value of cash flows	$25,000	–$1,036	–$ 942	–$ 856	–$ 779	–$4,433
Total present value of cash flows for purchase option = $16,954						
LEASE OPTION						
Lease	$6,000	$5,565	$5,565	$5,565	$5,565	0
Lease tax shield [3,4]	0	–1,800	–1,670	–1,670	–1,670	–1,670
Annual cash flow	6,000	3,765	3,895	3,895	3,895	–1,670
Present value factors [2]	×1	×.9091	×.8264	×.7513	×.6830	×.6209
Present value of cash flows	$6,000	$3,423	$3,219	$2,926	$2,660	–$1,037
Total present value of cash flows from lease option = $17,191						
Difference: apparent advantage of buying				$ 237		

[1] Depreciation expense × tax rate = depreciation tax shield
  Depreciation expense:
$$\frac{\$25,000 - \$6,000}{5} = \$3,800$$
$$\$3,800(0.30) = \underline{\$1,140}$$
[2] Discount factors are taken from Exhibit 8.1.
[3] $6,000(0.30) = \underline{\$1,800}$
[4] $5,565(0.30) = \underline{\$1,670}$

EXHIBIT 9.1. Discounted Cash Flow Payments Considering Tax Effects and Salvage Value

uses the straight-line method of depreciation. Exhibit 9.1 presents the effects of considering taxes and salvage value.

This time buying appears to be more advantageous than leasing by a mere $237. Note, however, that this is just an example based on assumptions. If the salvage value of the mower were somewhat lower, then the net result would probably favor leasing. On the other hand, a faster depreciation of the mower under the buy option might favor buying, and so on.

In addition, this example considers only the proposed lease without an option to buy the mower at a nominal price at the end of the lease period. Under many leases, especially capital leases, this option is available and will be considered in the second example below. When a golf course business is not subject to income tax, the approach is simply to compare the present value of the cash flows and select the alternative with the lowest cash outflow, as is also shown in the next example.

	Time, Years					
	0	1	2	3	4	5
PURCHASE OPTION						
Purchase price	$25,000					
Salvage value						−$6,000
Annual cash flows	25,000	0	0	0	0	− 6,000
Discount factors [(2)]	×1					×.6209
Present value of cash flows	$25,000					−$3,725
Total present value of cash flows for purchase option = $21,275						
LEASE OPTION						
Lease payments	$6,000	$5,565	$5,565	$5,565	$5,565	0
Nominal price						$1,000
Salvage value						−6,000
Annual cash flows	6,000	5,565	5,565	5,565	5,565	−5,000
Present value factors	×1	×.9091	×.8264	×.7513	×.6830	×.6209
Present value of cash flows	$6,000	$5,059	$4,599	$4,181	$3,801	−$3,105
Total present value of cash flows from lease option = $20,535						
Difference: apparent advantage to leasing				$ 740		

EXHIBIT 9.2. Discounted Cash Flow Payments—Capital Lease vs. Purchase Options

Exhibit 9.2 includes a second example, which compares the discounted cash flows of a capital lease and a purchase. The example is the same as shown in Exhibit 9.1 except for the following:

✦ Taxes are not considered in this example.

✦ The assumed purchase price at the end of the lease period is a nominal amount of $1,000. In this example, leasing is preferred by $740.

These are merely two examples used for illustrative purposes to present a systematic way of carefully comparing the alternative costs of leasing and buying equipment. Each example will result in different numbers, yet the process of evaluation is the same.

SIMPLE APPLICATION

Exhibit 9.3 is a quote from a Deere dealer for a John Deere 3215B Fairway Mower. The alternatives are as follows:

Purchase cost:	$30,591
True lease for 36 months:	$705.43/month
Lease/purchase for 36 months:	$964.23/month

Assumptions

The costs of maintenance are the responsibility of the ABC Golf Course, regardless of how the fairway mower is acquired. We will assume the mower will have a salvage value of $10,000 at the end of three years. Furthermore, to simplify the illustration assume the ABC Golf Course is a not-for-profit organization so income taxes can be ignored. In addition, the discount factor will be 12 percent on an annual basis, or 1 percent monthly.

What should Joe Superintendent of the ABC Golf Course do?

Based on the analysis of the annual cash flows for the three options, it appears Joe should select the true lease option. Exhibit 9.4 reveals the present value of cash flows for this option is $21,451.14, compared to $22,202.88 for the lease/purchase option and $23,473 for the purchase.

The major assumptions in this illustration are the discount rate and the salvage value. If these change significantly, the analysis will reveal a different decision.

WEINGARTZ SUPPLY CO., INC.

GOLF and TURF

August 28, 2003

ABC Golf Course
Joe Superintendent
123 Golf Lane
Anywhere, MI 48000
Fax: 555-GOLF

Dear Joe:

We are pleased to quote on the following equipment for your consideration.

Quan	Model #	Description	Unit Price	Total Price
1	1662M	John Deere 3215B Fairway Mower	$30,591.00	$ 30,591.00
		31.5 hp Fairway Traction Unit		
	4000	2 Wheel Drive		
	1025	(5) 7 Blade Heavy Section Cutting Units		
	2045	(5) 3" Spiral Design Self Cleaning Rollers		
		List Price	$36,425.00	

36 Month True Lease Monthly Payment	$705.43
36 Month Lease/ Purchase $1.00 Buyout Monthly Payment	$964.23

This quote is good for 30 days. Prices and payments do not include any applicable taxes.

Respectfully Submitted,

Joe Salesman

EXHIBIT 9.3

Purchase Option

Cost	$30,591
Salvage Value (three years hence)	
10,000 ×0 .7118[1]	<7,118>
Present value of cash flows	$23,473

True Lease Option

Initial monthly payment	$ 705.43
Future lease payments (present value)	
705.43 × 29.4086 [2]	20,745.71
Present value of cash flows	$21,451.14

Lease/Purchase Option

Initial monthly payment	$ 964.23
Future lease payments (present values)	
964.23 × 29.4086 [2]	28,356.65
Salvage value (present value) [3]	<7118.00>
Present value of cash flows	$22,202.88

[1] Present value factor 12%/three years
[2] Present value factor 1%/35 months

$$\text{Present value factor} = \frac{1 - \dfrac{1}{(1+i)^n}}{i}$$

i = discount factor of 1%
n = 35 months
[3] This assumes the $1 is paid and the mower could be sold for $10,000. The $1 payment is ignored to simplify the present value calculations.

EXHIBIT 9.4. Analysis of Purchase/Lease Options

SUMMARY

Leasing is an alternative to purchasing equipment. A lease is an agreement conveying the right from the lessor to the lessee to use resources.

Leases are accounted for as either capital or operating leases. When a lease is accounted for as a capital lease, the present value of the future minimum lease payments is recorded as an asset and as a liability. Expense is recognized over the life of the lease as depreciation. A lease accounted for as an operating lease results in a charge to equipment rent expense with each payment.

The major advantages of leasing, rather than financing a purchase of the item leased, are (1) working capital is conserved, (2) less red tape may be involved, and (3) quicker changes in equipment are possible when equipment becomes obsolete. Major disadvantages of leasing, rather than financing the purchase of the item leased, include (1) the loss of any residual value of the leased item, and (2) the difficulty in early termination of some leases.

To determine whether it is better to lease or buy a piece of equipment, the superintendent must calculate the total cost of each alternative. Consider the time value of money with lease payments and, when necessary, the tax effects of both options, as illustrated in Exhibit 9. 1.

PROBLEMS

Problem 1

The Forest Edge Course is considering the lease or purchase of a computer system and software for its superintendent. The purchase price is $12,000, while the lease payment for a five-year period is $3,000 at the beginning of each year. Assume that the expected useful life of this system is five years and that the system is expected to be worthless at the end of the five-year period.

Required:
1. What is the total cash outlay for each option?
2. What additional information is required to determine which option is preferred?

Problem 2

The golf course superintendent of the Waverly Golf Course (owned by the City of Lansing) is considering leasing or purchasing a fairway mower. Relevant information is as follows:

Purchase Option
        Purchase cost = $28,000
        Estimated salvage value = $6,000 (at end of useful life)
        Expected useful life = 5 years

Lease Option
        Initial lease payment at signing of lease = $7,000
        Future lease payments (due at the end of years 1 to 4) = $5,000

The relevant discount rate is 10 percent.

Required:
Based on the above information, determine whether the Waverly Golf Course should lease or buy.

MULTIPLE CHOICE QUESTIONS

1. The _____ is the party to a lease that owns the equipment, while the _____ is the party leasing the equipment.
   a. lessor; lessee
   b. lessee; lessor
   c. lessee; lessee
   d. lessor; lessor

2. An advantage of leasing equipment versus borrowing and purchasing the equipment is _____.
   a. working capital is generally conserved
   b. there generally is less paperwork with the lease
   c. it is often easy to get rid of an obsolete item
   d. all of the above

3. In considering whether to lease or buy, a superintendent must consider _____.
   a. the cost of the item
   b. the total lease payments
   c. the timing of all cash payments
   d. all of the above

4. A utility tractor costs the Alpha Golf Club $25,000. The club chose to pay $10,000 down and then make three annual cash payments of $6,000 each. The amount of interest paid by this club is _____.
   a. $0
   b. $3,000
   c. $5,000
   d. none of the above

5. The salvage value of a new mower (5 years hence) is estimated to be $5,000. The relevant discount rate is 10 percent. In comparing the costs of leasing versus buying, the amount to use for salvage value is _____.
   a. $0
   b. $3,105
   c. $5,000
   d. none of the above

Appendix

Solutions to Problems

Chapter 2

Multiple Choice

    1. d   2. b   3. c   4. d   5. d

Problem 1

Income Statement
Par More Course
For the Month of May

Green fees	$28,000
MGS sales	4,000
Driving range sales	1,500
Total revenues	33,500
Expenses	
Salaries and wages expenses	14,000
Payroll taxes and benefits	2,000
Supplies expense	3,000
Energy costs	1,500
Repairs expense	500
Interest expense	3,500
Depreciation expense	2,000
Income before Income Taxes	7,000
Income Taxes	2,100
Net Income	$ 4,900

Problem 2

Balance Sheet
Doe's Course
December 31, 20X1

ASSETS	
Current Assets	
Cash	$ 15,000
Accounts receivable	10,000
Inventories	6,000
Prepaid insurance	1,000
Total current assets	32,000
Investments	50,000
Property and Equipment	
Land	150,000
Buildings	400,000
Equipment	200,000
Total	750,000
Less: Accumulated depreciation	(200,000)
Net property and equipment	550,000
Total Assets	$632,000

LIABILITIES AND OWNER'S EQUITY	
Current Liabilities	
Accounts payable	$ 8,000
Wages payable	3,500
Taxes payable	3,000
Mortgage payable—current	40,000
Total current liabilities	54,500
Long-Term Liabilities	
Mortgage payable	320,000
Total Liabilities	374,500
Owner's Equity: R. Doe, Capital	257,500
Total Liabilities and Owner's Equity	$632,000

Chapter 3

Multiple Choice

1. b   2. d   3. c   4. c   5. d

Problem 1

1. Annual depreciation $= \dfrac{\text{Cost} - \text{Salvage value}}{\text{Life in years}}$

   Annual depreciation $= \dfrac{25{,}000 - 2{,}000}{5}$

   Annual depreciation $= \underline{\underline{\$4{,}600}}$

2. Annual depreciation $= (\text{Cost} - \text{Salvage value})\left(\dfrac{RL}{n(n+1)\,/\,2}\right)$

   Annual depreciation $= (25{,}000 - 2{,}000)\left(\dfrac{5}{5(5+1)\,/\,2}\right)$

   Annual depreciation $=\ 23{,}000(0.333)$

   Annual depreciation $= \underline{\underline{\$7{,}667}}$

3. There is no difference, as the total depreciation over the five-year period is $23,000 using each method.

Problem 2

1. Regular pay rate $= \dfrac{\text{Gross pay}}{\text{Hours worked}}$

   Regular pay rate $= \dfrac{300}{40} = \underline{\underline{\$7.50}}$

2. Overtime pay rate $=\ $ regular pay rate $\times\ 1.5$

   Overtime pay rate $=\ \$7.50 \times 1.5\ =\ \underline{\underline{\$11.25}}$

3.　Gross wages　=　(40 hours × $7.50) + (10 overtime hours × $11.25)

　　Gross wages　=　300　+　112.50　　　　　= $412.50

　　FICA　=　7.65% of gross wages　　　　　= $ 31.56

　　Federal withholding　=　20% of gross wages　= $ 82.50

　　State withholding　=　5% of gross wages　= $ 20.63

　　Net pay　=　gross　−　tax withholding　= $277.81

4.　Wages expense (24 × $7.50)　　　　$180.00
　　FICA expense ($180.00 × 0.0765)　$ 13.77
　　　　　　Wages payable　　　　　　　　　　　$180.00
　　　　　　Taxes payable　　　　　　　　　　　$ 13.77

To accrue unpaid wages and related taxes at the end of June.

Chapter 4

Multiple Choice

　　1. c　　2. d　　3. c　　4. b　　5. a

Problem 1

Horizontal Analysis, Riverview Club

	20X5	20X6	Dollar Difference	Percentage Difference
Departmental Expenses				
Payroll and related expenses:				
Salaries and wages	$180,000	$190,000	$10,000	5.6
Payroll taxes and benefits	40,000	45,000	5,000	12.5
Total	220,000	235,000	15,000	6.8
Other Expenses				
Supplies	80,000	85,000	5,000	6.3
Repairs	25,000	22,000	−3,000	−12.0
Energy costs	20,000	22,000	2,000	10.0
Other	10,000	12,000	2,000	20.0
Total	135,000	141,000	6,000	4.4
Total Golf Course Maintenance Expenses	$355,000	$376.000	$21,000	5.9

Problem 2

**Vertical Analysis, Hilltop Golf Enterprise
Golf Course Operations for the Month of May 20X6**

	Amounts	Percentages
Departmental Expenses		
Payroll and related expenses:		
Salaries and related expenses	$20,000	49.3%
Payroll taxes and employee benefits	5,000	12.3
Total payroll and related expenses	25,000	61.6
Other Expenses		
Ground and green supplies:		
Fertilizer and topsoil	4,000	9.8
Insecticides	1,000	2.5
Gasoline and lubricants	300	0.7
Sand and cinders	200	0.5
Seeds, flowers, plants, and shrubs	2,000	4.9
Other supplies	300	0.7
Other operating expenses	900	2.2
Repairs:		
Course buildings	500	1.2
Fences and bridges	200	0.5
Mowers, tractors, and trucks	3,500	8.6
Roads and paths	200	0.5
Water and drainage systems	1,800	4.4
Uniforms	200	0.5
Water and electricity	500	1.2
Total other expenses	15,600	38.4
Total Golf Course Maintenance Expenses	$40,600	100%

Chapter 5

Multiple Choice

    1. c   2. a   3. c   4. b   5. a

Problem 1

1. Current ratio (20X6) $= \dfrac{\text{Current assets}}{\text{Current liabilities}}$

    Current ratio $= \dfrac{\$60,000}{\$35,000} = \underline{\underline{1.71}}$

2. Debt/Equity (20X6) $= \dfrac{\text{Total debt}}{\text{Total owners' equity}}$

    Debt/Equity $= \dfrac{\$985,000}{\$2,115,000} = \underline{\underline{46.57\%}}$

3. Profit margin ratio $= \dfrac{\text{Net income}}{\text{Total revenues}}$

    Profit margin ratio $= \dfrac{\$60,000}{\$1,500,000} = \underline{\underline{4\%}}$

4. Return on total assets $= \dfrac{\text{Net income}}{\text{Average total assets}}$

    Return on total assets $= \dfrac{\$60,000}{\dfrac{(\$3,000,000 \ + \ 3,100,000)}{2}} = \underline{\underline{1.97\%}}$

5. Return on owners' equity $= \dfrac{\text{Net income}}{\text{Average owners' equity}}$

    Return on owners' equity $= \dfrac{\$60,000}{(1,970,000 \ + \ \$2,115,000) \ / \ 2} = \underline{\underline{2.94\%}}$

Problem 2

1. *The club's changing liquidity*

   The current ratio—an overall measure of liquidity—is increasing each year. This suggests that liquidity is increasing. The accounts receivable turnover, which focuses on receivables, is also a liquidity ratio. The declining turnover suggests that receivables are probably increasing each year. Though this may be good from a sales or use of the course perspective, receivables are not cash, and must be collected. Since receivables are less liquid than cash and temporary investments, the increase in receivables is viewed as being negative. Thus the overall increase in liquidity must be tempered by the apparent increase in a lesser liquid component of the current assets.

2. *The club's changing profitability*

   Comments on each ratio trend are as follows:

   a. Profits compared to average total assets are increasing, suggesting a greater profitability in using the club's total assets.
   b. Profits compared to total revenues are increasing, suggesting a more efficient operation overall.
   c. Profit compared to owners' equity is declining, suggesting a lower return on the owners' investment.

Chapter 6

Multiple Choice

1. a   2. b   3. c   4. b   5. d

Problem 1

1. Monthly breakeven:

$$X = \frac{\text{Fixed costs}}{\text{Greens fees} - \text{Variable costs per round}}$$

$$X = \frac{\$60,000}{\$12 - \$2} = 6,000$$

2. Annual breakeven

$$X = \frac{\$720,000}{\$12 - \$2} = 72,000$$

3. Necessary rounds to yield a profit

$$X = \frac{\$720{,}000 + \$50{,}000}{\$12 - \$2} = 77{,}000$$

Problem 2

1. Breakeven point:

$$X = \frac{\text{Cost of project}}{\text{Car rental} - \text{Variable costs per rental}}$$

$$X = \frac{\$160{,}000}{\$6 - \$2} = 40{,}000$$

2. Time to breakeven:

$$\text{Time in days} = \frac{\text{Car rentals to break even}}{\text{Average car rentals per day}}$$

$$\text{Time in days} = \frac{40{,}000}{100} = 400 \text{ golfing days}$$

Chapter 7

Multiple Choice

1. c   2. d   3. a   4. c   5. d

Problem 1

1. Forecast revenue for 20X7:

Greens fees:		
Rounds 42,000 + 0.05(42,000)	=	44,100
Greens fees		× $13
Total		573,300
Rental income (no change)		10,000
Total revenue		$583,300

2. Labor costs for 20X7:

Salaries and wages:
Fixed: 220,000 + 0.08(220,000) = $237,600
Variable: 44, 100 × 1.10 =   48,510
                        Subtotal   286,110
Benefits and payroll taxes:
Total salaries and wages $286,110
                          × 0. 16   45,778
        Total $331,888

Problem 2

1. Budget variances for wages expense

Actual $6,820
Budget   6,000
      Budget variance $ 820 (u)

2. Variance analysis

Usage variance:
$$UV = AR(BU - AU)$$
$$UV = 6.20(1{,}000 - 1{,}100)$$
$$UV = \underline{\$620}\ (u)$$

Rate variance:
$$RV = BH(BR - AR)$$
$$RV = 1{,}000(6 - 6.20)$$
$$RV = \underline{\$200}\ (u)$$

3. *Possible* causes of variances:

a. Usage variance
  (1) weather problems
  (2) more rounds played than anticipated
  (3) labor turnover in excess of plans, resulting in less efficient
      workers, thus more hours worked
b. Rate variance
  (1) overtime hours
  (2) wage increases in excess of plans
  (3) different staffing, resulting in larger percentage of higher
      hourly paid employees than planned

Chapter 8

Multiple Choice

1. b   2. c   3. b   4. a   5. b

Problem 1

Payback period:
    Cost of project: <u>$20,000</u>

Annual cash flow:	
Annual maintenance	<$2,000>
Elimination of vandalism	4,000
Increased play	<u>2,000</u>
Net cash flow	<u>$ 4,000</u>

Payback period: $\dfrac{\text{Cost of project}}{\text{Annual net cash flow}}$

Payback period: $\dfrac{\$20,000}{\$4,000} = 5$ years

Problem 2

1. Annual net cash flows:

Increased maintenance	<$ 5,000>
Increased greens fees	20,000
Increased food sales (net)	2,000
Increased misc. sales (net)	<u>2,000</u>
Total	<u>$19,000</u>

2. Net present value

Annual cash flow	$ 19,000
PV factor for an annuity 12%/10 years	×<u>5.6502</u>
Present value of cash flows	107,354
Less: construction cost	<u>50,000</u>
Net present value	<u>$ 57,354</u>

Chapter 9

Multiple Choice

    1. a   2. d   3. d   4. b   5. b

Problem 1

  1. Total cash outlay
          Purchase = \$12,000
          Lease = \$3,000 × 5 = \$15,000
  2. Other information:
     ✦ the discount factor to determine the present value of cash flows
     ✦ if Forest Edge is subject to taxes
        – the appropriate tax rate
        – the method of depreciation to be used

Problem 2

Present value of purchase option:

Cost	= \$ 28,000
Salvage value discounted to today:	
$6,000 × 0.6209	= <u><3,725></u>
Total	<u>\$24,275</u>

Present value of lease option:

Initial payment	= \$ 7,000
Future payments discounted to today:	
$5,000 × 3.1699	<u>15,850</u>
Total	<u>\$22,850</u>

Based on the above, leasing is preferred!

Index

Printed and bound by CPI Group (UK) Ltd, Croydon, CR0 4YY

23/04/2025

14660909-0001